# MODERN
# BOMBERS

# MODERN BOMBERS

An illustrated guide to bomber aircraft from 1945 to the second Gulf war, with 300 identification photographs

Featuring the Boeing B-52 Stratofortress, Panavia Tornado, Northrop Grumman B-2 Spirit stealth bomber, and many more ● **Francis Crosby**

**southwater**

*For Gemma.*
*Special thanks are due to Derek and*
*Marjorie Brammer for their considerable help*
*with research and administration.*

This edition is published by Southwater

Southwater is an imprint of Anness Publishing Ltd
Hermes House, 88–89 Blackfriars Road, London SE1 8HA
tel. 020 7401 2077; fax 020 7633 9499
www.southwaterbooks.com; info@anness.com

UK agent: The Manning Partnership Ltd, 6 The Old Dairy,
Melcombe Road, Bath BA2 3LR; tel. 01225 478444;
fax 01225 478440; sales@manning-partnership.co.uk

UK distributor: Grantham Book Services Ltd, Isaac Newton Way,
Alma Park Industrial Estate, Grantham, Lincs NG31 9SD;
tel. 01476 541080; fax 01476 541061; orders@gbs.tbs-ltd.co.uk

North American agent/distributor: National Book Network,
4501 Forbes Boulevard, Suite 200, Lanham, MD 20706;
tel. 301 459 3366; fax 301 429 5746; www.nbnbooks.com

Australian agent/distributor: Pan Macmillan Australia,
Level 18, St Martins Tower,
31 Market St,
Sydney, NSW 2000;
tel. 1300 135 113; fax 1300 135 103;
customer.service@macmillan.com.au

New Zealand agent/distributor: David Bateman Ltd,
30 Tarndale Grove, Off Bush Road,
Albany, Auckland;
tel. (09) 415 7664; fax (09) 415 8892

Publisher: Joanna Lorenz
Editorial Director: Judith Simons
Project Editor: Felicity Forster
Designer: Ian Sandom

Copy Editors: Judy Cox
and Jeremy Nichols
Editorial Reader: Rosanna Fairhead
Production Controller: Don Campaniello

Previously published as part of a larger volume, *Bombers*

1 3 5 7 9 10 8 6 4 2

PAGE 1: **BAE Systems Harrier.** PAGES 2–3: **Sepecat Jaguar.** BELOW: **BAC/BAE Strikemaster.**

# Contents

# Introduction

The earliest days of using aircraft as bombers saw pilots tossing small improvised bombs over the side of their aircraft on to a rather surprised enemy below. Hitting the target was more luck than judgement. This is a far cry indeed from the bomber aircraft of today that can fly around the world at several hundred miles an hour and arrive undetected in enemy airspace to drop precision-guided bombs down the chimney of a target and destroy it with no damage to surrounding buildings.

Once it was appreciated that the combination of aircraft and bombs was more than a novelty, military strategists were soon calling for more and bigger bombs to be carried. This required larger aircraft with more than one engine to carry the greater payload. Range then became an issue as the bombers had to be able to reach targets far beyond the front line. Engine technology and performance, as well as a greater understanding of aerodynamics, became considerations as the bombers had to be able to climb to heights away from enemy guns and fighters, or have sufficient speed to outrun the latter. Once the enemy started to try to knock the new bombers out of the sky, they had to defend themselves by carrying machine-guns and cannon. Technological advances saw the monoplane emerge, then largely replace the biplane in bomber fleets by World War II. Advances in construction techniques brought

ABOVE: **The General Dynamics F-111 was the first production aircraft in the world with "swing wings". These gave the aircraft the flexibility to land and take off with straight wings, but to fly at supersonic speeds with swept wings.**

## Key to flags

For the specification boxes, the national flag that was current at the time of the aircraft's use is shown.

**Brazil**

**France**

**Germany**

**Italy**

**United Kingdom**

**United States of America**

**USSR**

the use of more metal, specifically lightweight but strong alloys, and less wood and fabric. All-metal skins gradually replaced the fabric coverings of wings, fuselages and control surfaces.

The dawn of the jet engine opened up many opportunities for designers, but the long-range piston-engine bombers designed for use in World War II remained the mainstay of post-war bomber forces. Then, as atomic weapons appeared, bombers no longer had to carry many bombs at a time, because one atom bomb would do the same job.

During the Cold War, as the United States and the Soviet Union faced each other across thousands of miles of sea or polar ice caps, the priority was the development of aircraft that could fly as quickly as possible across the world to bomb the enemy. The Cold War fuelled bomber development after World War II, and most of the bomber aircraft in service around the world today were conceived during the Cold War. Large swept-wing jet bombers such as the Boeing B-47, Tupolev Tu-16, Boeing B-52 and Myasishchev M-4 were the principal bomber aircraft in the opposite inventories. All were good aircraft, but designers sought improvements in performance. The US B-58 Hustler was a Mach 2 nuclear bomber, but it proved to have insufficient range for the job required of it. Both Soviet and US engineers produced the brilliantly innovative variable-geometry designs with "swing wings" – the Tu-22M, F-111 and the B-1B. These aircraft, with wings spread, could cruise to their targets and then, with wings swept, could carry out high-speed, low-level attacks of which their larger fixed-sweep counterparts were simply not capable.

While bomber aircraft have evolved hugely since World War I, so have the weapons they can carry. "Dumb" free-fall conventional bombs are now complemented by "smart" munitions, which can be guided very precisely to a target. Bomber aircraft can also carry air-to-surface missiles, which were used in World War II, allowing them to attack a range of

TOP: **The Sukhoi Su-25 was first tested in battle during the Soviet invasion of Afghanistan in the early 1980s.** ABOVE: **A "smart" bomb being loaded on to an F-117A Nighthawk for Operation Desert Storm of the Gulf War, 1991.**

targets from a safe distance, such as troop concentrations, buildings, shipping or radar installations. Nuclear weapons remain an option for a number of nations around the world, but no weapon of this kind has been used in anger since the two raids on Japan in 1945.

The "stealth" aircraft currently in service with the US Air Force (F-117 and B-2) are remarkable examples of aviation technology, and were both produced as a result of the Cold War. Bomber aircraft became so sophisticated that people needed technological aids – radar – to find them. The designers of "stealth" aircraft have used technology to make the planes invisible again, creating the same surprise for the enemy that the manual bombing raids did in the early days of air warfare.

The performance figures quoted in this book should be seen as a broad indicator of an aircraft's capabilities. Aircraft performance and capability can vary considerably even within the same marks of an aircraft type. If bombs are carried, for example, maximum speed can be reduced. Also, the maximum speeds quoted are top speeds achieved at the optimum altitude for that particular aircraft type, and should not be seen as the definitive top speed for the aircraft at all altitudes.

ABOVE: **The futuristic-looking and adventurous delta-winged Avro Vulcan of the Royal Air Force, nicknamed the "tin triangle", first went to war in the Falkland Islands in 1982. It was extremely popular at air shows all over the world.**

# The History of Modern Bombers

From the early improvised bombers of World War I to the atomic bombers that ended World War II, and their successors which arguably kept peace during the Cold War, bomber aircraft have been a potent weapon at military leaders' disposal. Bombers evolved from slow short-range machines carrying light bomb loads through to the mighty B-52 Stratofortress which can fly around the world unrefuelled while carrying an enormous amount of weaponry, including "smart" bombs and cruise missiles. The latest generation of bomber aircraft are the "stealth aircraft" which can pass undetected through the most complex air defence systems.

While high speed and high altitude were once the aim of bomber designers, making maximum use of technology is now their goal. Total obliteration of the enemy is no longer the sole aim of bomber aircraft. We live in a very different world to that of almost a century ago when the first bombers lumbered into the air. Television beams live pictures of bombing raids into our homes and every mission can unleash a political storm. "Smart" precision weapons are therefore widely used to minimize avoidable loss of life and collateral damage.

LEFT: **Lockheed P2V Neptune.**

# Bomber aircraft development since World War II

The effectiveness of heavy bomber campaigns during World War II and the use of the ultimate weapon, the atomic bomb, meant that from the end of the war until the end of the 1950s, the heavy bomber was central to the military planning of the world's most powerful nations. The protagonists on the world stage were desperate to get a technological edge in case the Cold War ever heated up. Massive retaliation and mutually assured destruction awaited the players in a World War III unless new technology could provide one side with the upper hand and a means of total defeat of the enemy. The period was typified by major investment in experimental programmes, from flying wings to flying saucers. After the war, swept-wing jet bomber aircraft gradually replaced straight-wing piston-powered types, although turboprop bombers remain in front-line Russian service today in the form of the Tupolev Tu-95/142 "Bear" bomber/anti-submarine aircraft.

Greater knowledge of "area rule" (the design approach that produces a fuselage contour with the lowest possible transonic wave drag) came in the 1950s and helped engineers and aircraft designers beat the so-called "sound barrier" and produce aircraft capable of supersonic speeds in level flight. The quest for high speed was typified by the B-58 Hustler.

Jet engine technology progressed rapidly after the war. The Canberra B.2 was powered by the 2952kg/6500lb thrust Avon 101, while the B-47 had 3266kg/7200lb thrust J47-GE-25 turbojets. These bestowed a performance vastly better than the bombers in service just a few years previously. Compare that to the 13,980kg/30,780lb afterburning thrust of the B-1B Lancer's F-101 GE-102 turbofans. Afterburning or reheat capability was developed in the late 1940s to give jet-powered aircraft an emergency boost of energy when required.

The 1957 Soviet launch of the Sputnik satellite sent shockwaves through the Western world as everyone was quick to realize that if a satellite could be launched into space, an atomic device could also be launched using the same missile at London or Washington. There followed in the USA a crash programme in missile development, which culminated in a vast and potent missile arsenal in the USA. One result of this was that funding for the development of the manned bomber, which many thought was becoming a dinosaur, was a fraction

BELOW: **This photograph taken at Boeing's plant in Wichita, Kansas, shows B-47 Stratojets in final assembly. Development of this aircraft began before World War II ended. Stratojets entered USAF service in 1952, and were the USA's best nuclear deterrent in the period before ICBM missiles.**

LEFT: **The Panavia Tornado is one of the few variable-geometry or "swing-wing" aircraft to have entered front-line service. The Tornado has been the backbone of the Royal Air Force's bomber capability since the mid-1980s. This Tornado was pictured during the Gulf War, where the type specialized in daring and risky low-level attacks.** BELOW: **The Rockwell B-1 Lancer was designed to meet a mid-1960s requirement and, having survived cancellation, finally entered service in 1986. This was one of the last long-range strategic bombers to be built, and its impressive low-level high performance allows it to penetrate sophisticated air defences. While no true stealth technology was built into the B-1, it was designed with a small radar profile for such a large and capable aircraft.**

ABOVE: **The B-2 Spirit is a long-range strategic heavy bomber designed from the outset as a stealthy combat aircraft. It combines reduced infrared, acoustic, electromagnetic, visual and radar signatures, making the aircraft very hard to detect or track.** RIGHT: **A Lockheed F-117A Nighthawk "stealth fighter" under construction. This aircraft was the world's first to exploit low-observable stealth technology – its surfaces and edge profiles reflect hostile radar into narrow beam signals away from enemy radar detectors.**

of that spent on missile forces. Despite the presence of nuclear weapons in the world, which some people saw as a stabilizing factor, large and bloody wars continued to erupt around the world, and strategic bombers were not necessarily the best aircraft to have in the inventory.

The philosophy of massive retaliation seemed inflexible when what was needed was a flexible response, particularly for smaller conventional operations. This was a period of uncertainty in bomber history, and no bomber programmes were initiated and completed in the decade from 1960 to 1970.

Early jet bombers continued to use the materials and construction techniques of piston-powered aircraft. High-speed flight put extreme stresses on airframes,

so engineers looked beyond aluminium and magnesium alloys, and introduced titanium alloys and special steels. Carbon fibre composites are now widely used and are three times as strong while weighing half as much as aluminium alloys.

A truly innovative development of the post-war period was the swing or variable-geometry wing, in which the wings can move automatically from the swept to the spread position to maximize the aircraft's aerodynamic performance as required.

On take-off, the spread position generates more lift and gets the aircraft off the ground sooner. Once in the air, the wings sweep back for high-speed flight. Only a handful of swing-wing bombers, such as the F-111 and the Tornado, have seen service.

# Cold War bombers

Cold War rivalry and tensions between the United States/NATO and the Soviet Union/Warsaw Pact fuelled the development on both sides of more efficient and destructive bomber aircraft at almost any cost. Research, design and development were accelerated to a pitch that would have been unlikely had it not been for the Cold War.

In the immediate post-war period the Soviet Union's main bomber programme was the Tu-4, copied from US B-29s acquired during World War II. The Soviets reportedly spent two years carefully dismantling the US aircraft and studying the finest details of both structure and systems. The Tu-4 programme effectively kick-started Soviet post-war bomber development, the helping hand unwittingly given to them by their ideological enemies of the next four decades. The Soviet B-29 copies were produced from 1945 until 1953.

The years of the Cold War saw each side making a technological leap and the other mirroring or trying to improve the aircraft available should World War III have erupted. It was equally important to devise ways of countering new bombers through developing higher-performance fighters, early-warning and anti-aircraft technology,

> "It is an ironic, but accurate fact, that the two strongest powers are the two in the most danger of devastation."
> John F. Kennedy, June 10, 1963

ABOVE: **Royal Air Force Meteor fighters formating on and refuelling from a USAF Boeing KB-29 tanker converted from a standard B-29. Inflight refuelling was a vital means of extending the reach of Cold War combat aircraft – both fighters and bombers. Co-operation of this kind between the USAF and the RAF was common throughout the Cold War, and continues to this day.**

and specifically surface-to-air missiles. The USA usually took the lead, but there were some notable exceptions.

The priority for the USA was to develop a bomber that could strike around the world without the need for forward bases. They wanted the ability to fight the Soviet Union even if Europe fell and they had to launch strikes from the continental USA. The Soviet aim was also to reach its enemy from the other side of the world. One bomber that almost met this requirement, needing only one mid-air refuelling, was the English Electric Canberra-derived Martin B-57. However, the aircraft could not carry the large weapon load required over such vast distances.

Range was not enough: the aircraft also had to be able to avoid the unwelcome attentions of defending fighters by flying either higher or faster, or both. The B-36 had a top speed of 661kph/411mph, which was slower than many fighters of the World War II era. The answer for the USA came in the form of the B-47 Stratojet, Boeing's swept-wing, six-jet-engined design. The Tu-16, which used technology derived directly from the B-29, was the Soviet equivalent of the B-47 Stratojet, both of them first-generation swept-wing jet bombers.

Moscow's 1954 May Day parade fly-past saw the public debut of the Myasishchev M-4 long-range strategic bomber, which gave the Soviets the reach to hit the USA. The mighty Boeing B-52 Stratofortress had had its maiden flight a year earlier and in it the USAF finally got a high-performance bomber with intercontinental range. By the 1960s there were many experts who considered the bomber to be obsolete because new, highly accurate and destructive long-range missiles became available on both sides of the Iron Curtain. Despite this, bomber development continued, not just in the USA and the Soviet Union. Britain's V-bomber force included the highly advanced and complex Vulcan and Victor jet bombers which, although not having intercontinental range, could, with air-refuelling, have reached targets very far away from the UK. Similarly, France's Force de Dissuasion, equipped with high-speed Mirage IV bombers, was created as a potent deterrent against would-be aggressors.

ABOVE: **A picture considered impossible during the Cold War – a USAF B-52 Stratofortress parked near a Tupolev Tu-95 "Bear". These two very different bomber types faced each other across an ideological divide that lasted decades.**

BELOW: **Two classic British bomber types: a Handley Page Victor converted for tanker duties refuels two Blackburn Buccaneers. The Victor was in RAF service as a bomber from 1958 until the late 1970s. The Buccaneer, technically the last-ever all-British bomber, served in the Royal Navy and Royal Air Force from 1960 into the early 1990s.** BOTTOM: **The French were keen to develop their own nuclear deterrent and created the French Strategic Air Command's Force de Dissuasion. Equipped with the potent and high-performance Mirage IV, the force was ready for action around the clock from 1964 to 1996. Here, a Mirage IV refuels from a dedicated KC-135FR tanker.**

In the Tupolev Tu-22M, the Soviet Union created the first swing-wing strategic bomber, a major development. The American equivalent, the Rockwell B-1 project, was cancelled because of fears of rising costs. The Rockwell design was resurrected, and entered service as the highly capable B-1B Lancer. The development in bombers which really did take design into a new age was the unveiling of the Northrop B-2 Spirit, the "stealth bomber", believed to be the most expensive aircraft ever. Inspired by the Northrop Flying Wings of the 1940s, the B-2 was conceived during the Cold War as a long-range heavy bomber that could penetrate the world's most sophisticated air defences undetected and then drop up to 16 nuclear bombs. Aircraft such as the B-2 and the B-52 will be flying for many years to come. In the case of the B-52, the aircraft is expected to remain in service until 2045, a century after the start of the "war" for which it was designed to fight.

BELOW: **The Rockwell B-1 was conceived at the height of the Cold War, but is expected to stay in the front line for many years to come. The type saw extensive action during the 2003 war in Iraq.**

# Strategic Air Command

Strategic Air Command (SAC) was established in the USA on March 21, 1946, and in October that year its mission was defined: SAC was to attain an immediate state of combat readiness and to stand by for immediate operations, either alone or jointly with other forces, against enemies of the USA. In addition, SAC was required to develop, test and improve strategic bombardment tactics. Together with Tactical Air Command, SAC formed the offensive element of the USAF that existed for more than four decades.

On October 19, 1948, Lt. General Curtis E. Le May took command of SAC and went on to build it into the most powerful military force ever. Survivability was key to SAC's deterrence capability, so Le May moved the SAC Headquarters to the remote Offutt Air Force Base, Nebraska. SAC personnel were in no doubt as to the importance of their mission when Le May told them, "We are at war now!" Le May's aim was to build SAC into a force that could unleash such firepower and destruction on an enemy that they would no longer have the will or ability to wage war.

After slow development, the advent of the Korean War brought more funds to the USAF, enabling SAC to expand rapidly. Another driving factor in the development of SAC was the growing threat of Soviet military development, principally in the development of the Soviet hydrogen bomb, which was first tested on August 12, 1953.

To reduce the risk to its aircraft from enemy attack, SAC began to disperse them to bases across the USA, and did not have too many concentrated at a single location. In addition, SAC began acquiring bases around the world (in England, Greenland and Spain, among other locations) to improve its aircraft's ability to reach enemies anywhere.

BELOW: **The B-52, one of the greatest combat aircraft ever built, was the aircraft Le May was waiting for. Its entry into service in 1955 gave SAC the ability to fly around the world, strike at targets and fly home again. Although it was designed as a nuclear bomber, the Vietnam War showed the B-52's capabilities as a conventional bomber.**

LEFT: **This fine comparison shows the relative size of two of SAC's earliest bombers, the B-29 Superfortress (left) and the B-36 Peacemaker. The B-36 was the largest bomber ever to serve with the USAF, and for a decade in the late 1940s and early '50s, the Peacemaker provided SAC with a long-range strategic bomber deterrent.** BELOW: **Taken in October 1955, this photograph shows two RB-47s, the reconnaissance variant of SAC's Stratojet bomber.**

ABOVE: **A SAC KB-50 tanker refuelling an F-101 Voodoo, the fighter conceived as a long-range escort fighter for SAC B-36s. Voodoos would never have the range to go all the way with the bombers, but a range of 2414km/1500 miles still made it a useful defence.** RIGHT: **The B-58 Hustler joined SAC as a supersonic replacement for the B-47 Stratojet. In 1960, the B-58 became SAC's first operational supersonic bomber.**

Initially equipped with tired World War II aircraft types, by the mid-1950s SAC was operating its first all-jet bomber, the B-47 Stratojet. By 1955, SAC was being equipped with the mighty B-52 (still the backbone of the USAF bomber force around half a century later), the B-58 Hustler and, equally importantly, the KC-135 jet tanker, which gave SAC a truly global reach. SAC demonstrated its ability to strike anywhere around the world when three B-52s made a non-stop round-the-world flight. By the late 1950s, SAC was complementing its airborne nuclear forces with ballistic nuclear missiles.

By 1960, a third of SAC's bombers and tankers were on 15-minute ground alert, combat-ready and armed for nuclear war. By July 1961, half of SAC's bombers and tankers were on ground alert while a number of nuclear-armed bombers were constantly airborne. From February 1961, SAC kept an

Airborne Command Post in the air at all times, ready to take control of SAC forces in the event of an attack on the SAC HQ at Offut. From 1964 to 1973, SAC bombers flew thousands of bombing missions in South-east Asia, and the Linebacker II campaign in December 1972 is thought to have brought the North Vietnamese back to the peace table.

The collapse of the Soviet Union at the end of the Cold War brought an end to the threat of Soviet aggression. Following the Gulf War in 1991, a restructuring of the United States Air Force brought the stand-down of Strategic Air Command. On June 1, 1992, Strategic Air Command passed into the history books, hailed by many as the winner of the Cold War.

# Bomber aircraft defences from 1945

Most of the bombers in service in the post-war period had some type of defensive gun armament. B-29s, like their B-17 predecessors, bristled with guns in tail, waist and ventral positions. In the late 1940s and early '50s it was felt that, provided a bomber could fly higher and faster than defending fighters and anti-aircraft fire, it would get to its target unscathed. This was the philosophy behind the wartime de Havilland Mosquito and the jet-powered English Electric Canberra which first flew in 1949 – in bomber configuration, neither type carried defensive armament.

Guns continued to be installed in bombers, although guns in nose positions were omitted as bomber aircraft began to fly higher and faster. The Avro Shackleton may well have been the last front-line bomber in service with this form of

armament. The B-52, however, did retain a group of remotely controlled cannon in the tail, which was only deleted in later versions. Even the high-speed Tupolev Tu-22M had two radar-controlled cannon in its tail. Today the backbone of Britain's bomber force, the Panavia Tornado GR4, has a 27mm/1.05in cannon in the nose.

World War II proved the value of fighter escort for large fleets of bombers, and this no doubt prompted the decision to trial a very unusual defensive installation in the B-36 Peacemaker. The B-36 was so large that its forward bomb

RIGHT: **Few aircraft have had the capability to carry another aircraft for defence, but Strategic Air Command's B-36 Peacemaker could. Trials with an F-85 Goblin were followed by more using an F-86 Thunderstreak.**
BELOW: **The structure of "stealth" aircraft, such as the Lockheed F-117 Nighthawk pictured, and the materials from which they are made, are central to their defence and survivability.**

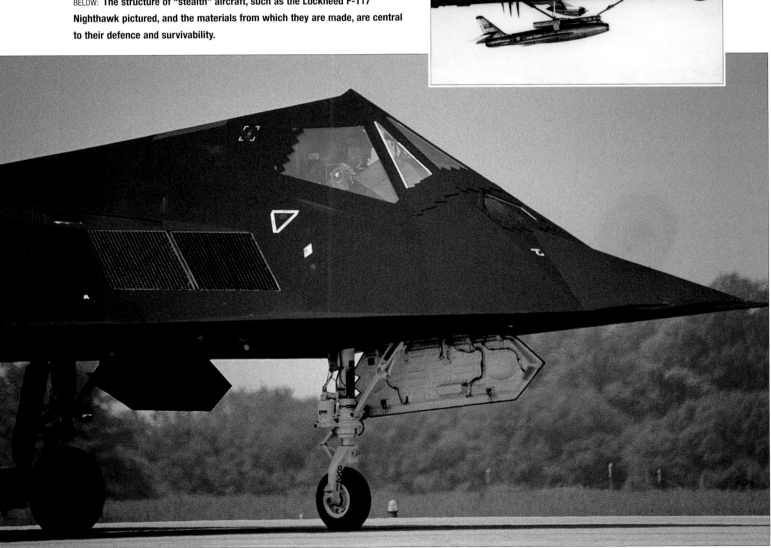

bay had room to carry a McDonnell F-85 Goblin jet fighter that could protect the bomber from enemy fighters and then return to the aircraft.

However, the unarmed Mosquito approach held good until anti-aircraft missile technology produced missiles that could down a jet aircraft at 18,300m/60,000ft. Most anti-aircraft missiles were fired at targets tracked on radar, which then directed the missile to the vicinity of the target. The missile would switch to its own homing facility and look for a heat source, normally the aircraft's engine jet pipe. The same technique was used by most air-to-air fighter-launched missiles. A hit from a missile was usually enough to bring down any aircraft – warheads varied from high explosive to "shrapnel" types, and some were even nuclear-tipped. Bombers began to employ various means of confusing would-be attackers. Radar-controlled missiles would only function if the radar could find and lock on to its target. Bombers carry electronic jamming devices which will find and jam the appropriate enemy fire control radars of anti-aircraft guns and missiles. On some missions, for example the Libya raids carried out by the USAF, dedicated jamming aircraft (EF-111s) went in ahead of the main attack force. During the RAF's Black Buck bombing raids on the Falklands, specialized Shrike anti-radar missiles were fired by Vulcan bombers.

Most bombers now carry special rear warning radar to alert crews to unwelcome attention from the rear. On-board equipment detects missile locks from fighter aircraft or missiles. The bomber can then take evasive action and deploy bundles of chaff (strips of metal foil) to create a confusing radar image, and also flares which fire 20 to 30 times around the aircraft, presenting a plethora of brilliantly hot, burning objects that hopefully draw the heat-seeking missile away.

"Stealth" aircraft revolutionized bomber operations because potential enemies at the time relied on defence radars to pick up incoming bombers. Most radars cannot pick up the stealth aircraft and, if they did, heat-seeking missiles would be thwarted thanks to the ingenious cooling and dissipation of hot exhaust gases from the aircraft's engines, which reduced the aircraft's infrared signature. All future bomber aircraft will be made using stealth technology.

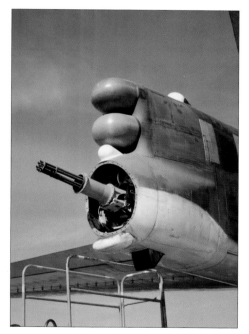

FAR LEFT: **In contrast to the hi-tech tail defences of the B-52, the Tu-95 Bear retains two 23mm/ 0.9in cannon in the tail which can be fired manually. The tail turret is clearly inspired by that of the Tu-4 B-29 copy produced in the Soviet Union in the years following World War II.** LEFT: **The tail of the B-52 has changed considerably during its time in service. It was initially armed with four remotely controlled 12.7mm/0.5in machine-guns. In the H-model pictured, the tail defence is the 20mm/0.78in "minigun", part of the AN/ASG-21 Defensive Fire Control system. Note also the tail warning and search radomes above the gun.**
BELOW LEFT: **Even the Mach 2-capable Panavia Tornado carries cannon armament in the nose.**
BELOW: **Avro Shackleton. The "Shack" was probably the last front-line bomber with nose guns.**

# V-bombers

**B**ritain's V-bombers – the Vulcan, Victor and Valiant – were the last of the Royal Air Force's long-range heavy bombers, and they were Britain's airborne nuclear deterrent from 1955 until 1968.

The concept of the force, not seen as one of mixed aircraft types at first, had its origins in a 1946 Air Ministry Operational Requirement calling for a bomber able to carry a 4542kg/ 10,000lb atomic bomb to a target 2775km/1725 miles away, from a base anywhere in the world. The aircraft was required to deliver its bomb deep into enemy territory and avoid destruction by enemy aircraft or anti-aircraft defences.

Four very different jet-powered designs from four different companies made it from the drawing board in response to the requirement. Avro and Handley Page both proposed futuristic, aerodynamically adventurous designs judged to be sufficiently risky that Vickers and Shorts were invited to develop their rather simpler and thus less risky designs as something of an insurance policy for the RAF. The Air Staff asked for the Vickers design, ultimately named Valiant, to be produced over the Short Sperrin as the interim aircraft, while the advanced Avro and Handley Page aircraft were developed into the Vulcan and Victor respectively. These aircraft represented a massive technological leap for an air force equipped with Lancasters, Lincolns and latterly old B-29s loaned by the

TOP: **XA901 was a Vulcan B.1 and was one of the earlier Vulcans to be produced. The total number of B.1s built was 45, the last delivered to the RAF in April 1959. The all-white, anti-flash paint scheme was intended to offer some protection against the effects of the flash following a nuclear detonation.** ABOVE: **Elements of the V-force were rotated overseas to Akrotiri in Cyprus, the location photographed here in 1970. From Cyprus, the bombers would have been able to reach targets beyond the range of UK-based aircraft. Beneath this Vulcan's nose is a tanker version of the Victor bomber.**

Americans. Looking back, it took surprisingly little time – only nine years – for the jet-powered nuclear bombers to reach squadron service.

The V-bombers were effectively designed around Britain's own atomic bomb, which was developed in parallel with the aircraft. Britain's first operational atomic bomb, "Blue Danube", a free-fall plutonium bomb, was available in November 1953, but it was not until 1955 that Britain's first atomic bomber unit, No.138 Squadron, was operational with its Valiants at RAF Wittering. Although the jet-powered Canberra had been in Bomber Command service since 1951, its bomb bay was too small to take the British A-bomb that became available.

It was January 1957 before the first Vulcans entered service with the RAF's 230 OCU (Operational Conversion Unit) at Waddington, and the type was entering squadron service by the summer. November 1957 saw the Victor deliveries beginning and the Handley Page bomber was in squadron use from April 1958. Ten RAF airfields were updated to become V-bomber bases, while a further 26 were earmarked as V-bomber dispersal bases in times of international tension.

The V-force possessed massive destructive capability, and its credibility as an effective deterrent against would-be aggressors – specifically the Soviet Union – rested on its ability to get airborne and get to the target if required. The V-force perfected the QRA (quick reaction alert), whereby a number of aircraft were fuelled, armed and ready to be airborne in just four minutes, the amount of time it would take for a detected Soviet ballistic missile to impact on UK bases. The credibility of the V-force was in question once Soviet anti-aircraft technology developed to the point that a U-2 spyplane was shot down over the USSR from an altitude of 19,810m/65,000ft in May 1960. The answer was to bring the V-force down to low level, operating below the effective height of most enemy radars, only climbing to an altitude of 3660m/12,000ft to drop the deadly cargo. By now the force was carrying the Yellow Sun hydrogen bomb, which was replaced by the WE177 weapon in the mid-1960s. Later-mark Victors and Vulcans were armed with the Blue Steel stand-off

TOP: **The enormous Blue Danube atomic bomb, around which the V-bombers were designed. This all-British weapon was a free-fall plutonium bomb.**
ABOVE: **The Vickers Valiant was the most conventional of the three V-bomber designs, and was ordered as insurance should the more advanced Victor and Vulcan be problematic.** BELOW: **The Victor first flew in prototype form just seven years after the end of World War II, yet this aircraft served in the RAF until 1993 when the last tanker versions were retired. The Victor could carry the greatest bomb load of the V-bombers, an impressive 15,890kg/35,000lb.**

missile with a range of 161km/100miles. This enabled the V-bombers to improve the launch aircraft's survivability over heavily defended targets.

When the strategic deterrent role passed from the V-force to the Royal Navy's Polaris submarines in 1969, these aircraft remained in front-line service (although the Valiant had been withdrawn by then) and were still very potent weapon platforms with the ability to carry many tons of bombs, including nuclear payloads, if required.

# The Falklands Black Buck raids

When Argentina invaded the Falklands in 1982, Britain's campaign to regain the islands was made more difficult because of the sheer distances involved. Once Britain's Task Force was ready to re-take the islands, Argentine air defences on the Falklands had to be disabled. Firstly, the runway at Port Stanley had to be made unusable for Argentine aircraft, as it was assumed that, given time, the Argentine air force would base Mirage and Skyhawk fighters there, which could have made things very difficult for the Task Force. Without a Falklands base, these combat aircraft operating from the Argentine mainland were near the limits of their operating radius. Secondly, Argentine radar sites had to be neutralized so that the British Harriers of the Task Force could not be attacked or detected. The missions had to take place in total secrecy from friendly territory which led the military planners to one choice: Ascension Island, a small British dependency in the Atlantic almost 6436km/4000 miles from the Falklands. There was only one aircraft in the RAF inventory that could carry a heavy bomb load over the considerable distances involved – the Vulcan.

TOP: **The Vulcan finally saw action after almost three decades of service when the type was used to carry out the longest bombing raids ever contemplated.**
ABOVE: **The raid was only possible with a complex series of inflight refuellings from Victor tankers which themselves had to be refuelled to get back to base.**

The missions to the Falklands were codenamed "Operation Black Buck", and five were ultimately flown. Three were directed against the runway at Stanley, while a further two attacked radar sites on the islands. The logistics of these missions are staggering, and with the distance from Ascension to the Falklands a 16-hour round trip of over 12,389km/7700 miles, they were at that point the longest bombing missions in history.

LEFT AND BELOW: **A key aim of the Black Buck missions was to put the Port Stanley runway out of action. This was essential to prevent its use by Argentine Mirage (left) and Skyhawk (below) aircraft which posed a significant threat to the British Task Force. Both were near the end of their range operating from the Argentine mainland, and they could be contained by the British Harriers.**

Each Black Buck Vulcan had to be refuelled numerous times by RAF Victor tankers also operating from Ascension, and some of the tankers themselves had to be refuelled to get home. Although many RAF Vulcans had refuelling probes, they had not been used for some time. There followed a period where serviceable refuelling probes were sought, one apparently coming from a Vulcan in a museum. Because of the great distances involved over the ocean, the Vulcans needed improved navigation aids, which came in the form of equipment allegedly acquired from a British Airways store. In addition, the Vulcan's throttle controls were modified to allow pilots unlimited power from the Olympus engines.

The first Black Buck mission took place from April 30 to May 1, 1982. Loaded with 21 x 454kg/1000lb bombs, two Vulcans took off from Ascension for the eight-hour trip to their target, escorted by no fewer than 11 Victor tankers which had to refuel the bombers or each other to reach the Falklands and return.

One of the Vulcans developed a technical problem and had to return to base, leaving a lone Vulcan – XM607 – to carry out the mission. Dwindling numbers of tankers flew on with the Vulcan while the empty tankers returned to Ascension, many with barely enough fuel to land. The last Victor transferred so

much fuel to the Vulcan that it only had enough left to get within 644km/400 miles of Ascension, and another Victor had to launch to refuel the incoming "dry" tanker.

About 482km/300 miles from Stanley, the Vulcan descended to 92m/300ft above the sea to avoid detection, and about 64km/40 miles out the aircraft climbed to 3050m/10,000ft to begin the bombing run. Then, 16km/10 miles from the target, an anti-aircraft gun radar was detected, but was jammed by equipment on the Vulcan supplied by the Americans. Twenty-one 454kg/1000lb bombs were dropped in a diagonal line across the runway, one hitting the runway dead-centre.

The effect of this and subsequent Black Buck raids was more on Argentine morale than the Argentine military machine. If Vulcans could reach the Falklands, they could reach the Argentine mainland and, as a result, many Argentine fighters were kept back to defend against a possible raid on Argentina. The raids had been a success.

LEFT: **XM607 was one of the Vulcan B.2s that carried out the Black Buck raids. Armed with 21 x 454kg/1000lb bombs, the Vulcan dropped the bombs obliquely across the runway. Argentina then feared that an attack on the mainland might also have been feasible.**

# Operation El Dorado Canyon

In 1986, following a number of terrorist attacks on US citizens and interests, US intelligence cited "incontrovertible" evidence that the incidents were sponsored by Libya. On April 14, 1986, the United States launched Operation El Dorado Canyon against Libya. Part of the operation called for UK-based USAF F-111 crews to fly one of the longest combat missions in history.

US President Ronald Reagan wanted to mount a strike against the regime of Libyan leader Colonel Gadaffi, but first sought cooperation from the Western Allies. The USAF's 48th Tactical Fighter Wing in England had been working on plans for a strike, which assumed that the F-111s could fly through French airspace to strike at Libya. Western media speculation about the strike caused the plan to be changed to include support aircraft (EF-111 and US Navy A-7 and EA-6B) to carry out the suppression of enemy defences. The US Navy role in the operation grew, as the raid had to hit Gadaffi hard.

Plans were further complicated when France, Germany, Italy and Spain all refused to cooperate in a strike. Only Britain cooperated by allowing the use of its soil to launch the attack. A radically different plan was drawn up. The F-111s would now navigate over the ocean around France and Spain, pass east over the Strait of Gibraltar and then over the Mediterranean to line up for their bombing run on Libya.

It would be a gruelling round trip of 10,298km/6400 miles, taking 13 hours and needing from eight to twelve inflight refuellings for each of the bombers. The F-111 crews, trained for missions against the Soviet Union, were familiar with 2-hour NATO sorties, so El Dorado Canyon placed a tremendous strain on the crews and the aircraft's complex systems.

RIGHT: **The map used by Secretary of Defense Weinberger at the White House briefing which told the world of Operation El Dorado Canyon.** BELOW: **An F-111 leaves the runway at RAF Lakenheath in Suffolk, England, to take part in what was then the longest bombing mission in history. The F-111 is a very fast and accurate low-level bomber, but the aircraft was not designed for gruelling 13-hour missions like the Libya raids.**

US planners tabled a joint USAF/USN attack against five major Libyan targets. Two were in Benghazi: a terrorist training camp and a military airfield. The other three targets were in Tripoli: a terrorist naval training base; the former Wheelus AFB; and the Azziziyah Barracks compound, which housed the HQ of Libyan intelligence and also contained one of five residences that Gadaffi was known to have used. Eighteen F-111s were to strike the Tripoli targets, while US Navy aircraft were to hit the two Benghazi sites.

At 17:36 GMT on April 14, 24 F-111s left Lakenheath, six of them spare aircraft set to return after the first refuelling. Five EF-111 electronic warfare aircraft also launched. This was the start of the first US bomber mission from British soil since the end of World War II. The US Navy attack aircraft came from carriers of the Sixth Fleet operating in the Mediterranean. Coral Sea provided eight A-6E medium bombers and six F/A-18C Hornets for strike support. America launched six A-6Es, plus six A-7Es and an EA-6B for strike support. They faced a hazardous flight because Libya's air defence system was virtually on a par with that of the Soviet Union. Timing was critical, and the USAF and USN attacks had to be simultaneous to maximize the element of surprise so that the strike aircraft could get in and out as quickly as possible.

Of the 18 F-111s that headed for Libya, five had aborted en route, so at around midnight GMT, 13 F-111s reached Tripoli. The first three elements hit the Azziziyah Barracks. One element struck the Sidi Balal terrorist training camp while the two remaining elements, armed with parachute-retarded 225kg/500lb bombs, struck Tripoli airport, destroying a number of aircraft in the process. The F-111s carried out their attack at speeds around 740kph/460mph and heights of 60m/200ft.

EF-111As and Navy A-7s, A-6Es, and an EA-6B armed with HARM and Shrike anti-radar missiles flew in defence suppression roles for the F-111s. Across the Gulf of Sidra, Navy A-6E aircraft attacked the Al Jumahiriya Barracks at Benghazi, and to the east the Benina airfield.

News of the attack was being broadcast in the USA while it was underway. One F-111 aircraft was lost over Tripoli, possibly hit by a SAM, and its crew were killed. The F-111s spent only 11 minutes in the area of the targets, then faced a long flight home with yet more inflight refuellings.

The operation was never intended to be a means of toppling Gadaffi, but he is known to have been very shaken when bombs exploded near him. When he next appeared on state television, he was certainly subdued. Most importantly, the raids demonstrated that even in those pre-"stealth" days, the USA had the capability to send its high-speed bombers over great distances to carry out precision attacks. The raid was considered a success, but the situation between the USA and Gadaffi remained unresolved until an uneasy peace was agreed 17 years later.

BELOW: **This photograph, taken on February 12, 1986, shows the deck of the USS *Saratoga* (CV-60) as flight-deck crews prepare EA-6B Prowlers, F-14 Tomcats and A-7 Corsairs for operations in the southern Mediterranean. Tension was high between the USA and Libya, and on March 24, 1986, the US Navy destroyed a SAM site after USN aircraft were targeted unsuccessfully by Libyan missiles.**

ABOVE: **A still from film taken by a USAF F-111 as the US attack on the military side of Tripoli airport begins. 225kg/500lb bombs were dropped on these Soviet-made Il-76 transports, which the USA believed transported military and subversive materials around the world. The film was shot at night using the F-111's Pave Tack laser-guided delivery system.** LEFT: **Photographs taken by US Navy aircraft on April 15, 1986 show the damage caused at Benina airfield by the previous day's attack carried out by USN aircraft.**

BENINA AIRFIELD
15 APR 86

DESTROYED MIG-23/FLOGGER

MIG-23/FLOGGER PIECES

# Gulf War bombers

The air campaign against Iraq was launched on January 16, 1991, the day after the United Nations' deadline for Iraqi withdrawal from Kuwait expired. Operation Desert Shield had become Desert Storm. The scale and strength of the Allied air attacks on one night were staggering, and the initial air attack removed much of Iraq's ability to defend itself against further air assaults. The air campaign was conducted by the USA, Saudi, British, French, Italian and Free Kuwaiti, as well as various Arab air forces.

Lockheed F-117 "stealth fighters" flew to the Iraqi capital of Baghdad and destroyed command and control centres. As Baghdad's anti-aircraft defences (seven times greater than that of Hanoi later in the Vietnam War) blazed away at targets it could not see, the F-117s were delivering 907kg/2000lb laser-guided bombs down ventilation shafts and through doorways to destroy underground bunkered facilities. Meanwhile, cruise missiles were also taking out targets with pinpoint accuracy. Seven USAF B-52Gs had taken off from Barksdale Air Force Base, Louisiana, and headed towards the Persian Gulf. They flew a round trip of more than 22,526km/14,000 miles, remaining airborne for 35 hours, the longest combat mission in history at that time. The launch of their Boeing AGM-86C conventionally armed cruise missiles (first combat use for the weapon) was one of the opening salvoes

TOP: **Operating from RAF Fairford in Britain, eight USAF B-52s dropped a total of 1176 tonnes/1158 tons of bombs during 60 missions on mainly front-line Republican Guard targets.** ABOVE: **The Republic A-10 Thunderbolt proved to be a modern equivalent of the Hawker Typhoon, carrying out much the same job as the "Tiffie" after D-Day, attacking enemy armour and vehicles. However, the Typhoon was not armed with the A-10's deadly 30mm/1.18in cannon which fires 30 armour-piercing rounds per second.**

of the operation. Iraqi anti-aircraft defences then became targets themselves with scores of US defence suppression types such as the EF-111, F-4G Wild Weasels and EA-6 Prowlers launching anti-radiation missiles or using powerful jammers to cripple enemy electronic sensors.

LEFT: **The crew of RAF Victor K2 tanker XH671 head out to their aircraft for another mission in support of Desert Storm combat aircraft. These flying petrol stations were essential for aircraft such as Tornados and Buccaneers.**
BELOW: **An F-111 of the UK-based 48th Tactical Fighter Wing "in theatre" at Taif in Saudi Arabia during the Gulf War. In 2500 Gulf War F-111 missions, these fine aircraft destroyed 2203 targets, including artillery, 13 runways, 245 hardened aircraft shelters and 12 bridges.**

For a month, Coalition aircraft pounded away at any targets that might contribute to the Iraqi ground war effort. Precision bombs were used to minimize errors and casualties – a successful strike was one that hit within 3m/10ft of its mark.

In the first day of Desert Storm, 655 Coalition aircraft flew 1322 sorties against communication centres and airfields. Within 24 hours, the Coalition achieved air superiority and was then at liberty to destroy Iraq's command and control centres, and to cut communications between Kuwait and Baghdad.

Once defences were silenced, strike aircraft, including the Jaguar, F-16 and F/A-18, hit airfield complexes with conventional bombs. RAF Tornado bombers specialized in the use of the devastating JP233 runway denial weapon system against Iraqi runways. This weapon had to be used at low level, which led to relatively high losses among the RAF bomber crews. Hardened shelters were not able to protect Iraqi aircraft hidden within because the Coalition bombers were able to direct pinpoint attacks on the structures' doors.

Veteran Royal Air Force Buccaneers, normally deployed in the maritime attack role in the UK, were rushed to the Gulf for overland laser designation (target-marking) missions. Armed with Sidewinder AAMs for self defence, pairs of Buccaneers

would operate with four Tornados, all carrying precision-guided bombs and the "Buccs" each carrying a laser pod – two were carried in case one became unserviceable, thus avoiding the entire mission

> **"We have carefully chosen our targets and we've bombed them with precision." US Secretary of Defense Dick Cheney, 1991**

being scrubbed. The Buccaneer flew the first such mission on February 2 against the As Suwaira road bridge. These mixed Tornado/Buccaneer teams destroyed 20 road bridges over the Tigris and Euphrates rivers, very effectively breaking Iraqi supply lines to their invasion forces in Kuwait. Unknown to the Coalition, the Iraqis had run their fibre optic communications cables along the bridges, so every wrecked bridge added to communications chaos among the enemy.

Allied Air Forces then proceeded to pound the Iraqi land forces – specifically the divisions deployed in Kuwait and Southern Iraq. The USAF's veteran B-52 bombers, operating mainly from Diego Garcia in the Indian Ocean, decimated the morale of Iraq's Republican Guard. They delivered some 40 per cent of all the weapons dropped by Coalition forces and flew approximately 1620 combat sorties.

Coalition bombers continued to attack Iraqi targets until the invaders were driven from Kuwait, and on March 3, 1991, Iraq accepted the ceasefire.

LEFT: **A Royal Air Force Tornado GR1 at its base in Kuwait. The Tornado played a vital strike role during the war, initially tasked with hazardous low-level missions. In all, 1500 bombing raids were carried out by the swing-wing bombers.**

# A–Z of Modern Bombers
## 1945 to the Present Day

The devastating atom bomb raids on Japan that brought World War II to a close guaranteed, at least for a time, the future development of bombers in nations developing such weapons for themselves. Atomic weapons would only be effective if an efficient means of delivery was available. As the Cold War began, the immediate need on all sides was for bomber aircraft that could travel considerable distances, outperform enemy defences and then bomb effectively. Jet technology and greater understanding of aerodynamics led to bomber aircraft flying higher and faster, up to twice the speed of sound. The Cold War forced the development of new technology in many directions, perhaps most spectacularly in "stealth".

By the late 1950s and early '60s, anti-aircraft defence developments, notably SAM missiles and the development of intercontinental ballistic missiles, called the very need for bombers into question. However, ongoing conventional warfare the world over has proved the need for aircraft that can be operated flexibly. Very high speed is no longer a prerequisite for bombers, whereas survivability in today's highly sophisticated air warfare environment is vital.

LEFT: **Lockheed F-117 Nighthawk.**

# Aermacchi MB-339

## Aermacchi MB-339C

**First flight:** August 12, 1976
**Power:** One licence-built Rolls-Royce 1998kg/
    4400lb thrust Viper 680-43 turbojet
**Armament:** Up to 1816kg/4000lb of external
    weapons including bombs, rockets, cannon
    pods, anti-shipping missiles and air-to-air
    missiles
**Size:** Wingspan – 11.22m/36ft 10in
    Length – 11.24m/36ft 11in
    Height – 3.99m/13ft 1in
    Wing area – 19.3m²/207.7sq ft
**Weights:** Empty – 3313kg/7297lb
    Maximum take-off – 6356kg/14,000lb
**Performance:** Maximum speed – 902kph/560mph
    Ceiling – 14243m/46,700ft
    Range – 2035km/1263 miles
    Climb – 9150m/30,000ft in 6 minutes, 40 seconds

The origins of the MB-339 advanced trainer/light attack aircraft date back to the mid-1950s when the hugely successful MB-326 trainer (and later light attack aircraft) was first designed. By the 1970s Aermacchi were considering a successor, and the MB-339 was born. The airframe shares a lot of its structure with the MB-326K light attack aircraft, with the forward fuselage redesigned to allow the tandem seating to be staggered vertically enabling the instructor to see over the pupil.

The resulting aircraft is stronger and has an uprated powerplant compared to the MB-326. Six hardpoints carrying up to 1816kg/4000lb give this nimble aircraft a powerful punch. The first prototype, I-NOVE, flew on August 12, 1976, and the first production MB-339A trainer was delivered to the Italian Air Force on August 9, 1979. Other customers included New Zealand, Argentina, Dubai, Ghana, Malaysia, Nigeria and Peru. Perhaps the most high-profile user of the MB-339 are the Italian Frecce Tricolori aerobatics display team.

The MB-339AM was a proposed maritime strike version, while the Viper 680-powered MB-339B is enhanced for the ground-attack role. The MB339-K (also known as the Veltro 2), was a single-seat attack version yet to be produced. The next ground-attack version was the MB-339C. Also powered by the Viper 680-43, this version first flew on December 17, 1985, and can carry air-to-air and air-to-ground missiles as well as bombs. The first production customer for the C-model was the Royal New Zealand Air Force, who received their first three aircraft in April 1991.

The MB-339 FD is the latest and most advanced version of the MB-339 in service, and is equipped with self-defence systems for more realistic operational training and for increasing the aircraft survivability in combat.

TOP: **A Royal New Zealand Air Force MB-339. The advanced trainer was seen by many nations as a means of acquiring cost-effective ground-attack capability.** ABOVE: **MB-339Cs.** BELOW: **An Italian Air Force MB-339A.**

LEFT: **A Brazilian Air Force AMX performing a ground-attack demonstration. The aircraft is a fine example of technological and manufacturing co-operation between two nations thousands of miles apart.** BELOW: **The International AMX-T two-seat version.**

# AMX International AMX

The AMX fighter-bomber originated from a requirement from the Italian Air Force for a ground-attack aircraft to replace its G91 and F-104s, and the Brazilians' need to replace their MB-326s.

A special consortium was set up to produce this very capable aircraft in both Italy and Brazil. Italian companies Alenia and Aermacchi produce around 70 per cent of the aircraft and Brazilian company Embraer is responsible for 30 per cent. Alenia manufactures the central section of the fuselage, radome, ailerons, spoilers and tail surfaces. Aermacchi is responsible for the forward fuselage, integration of the guns (one 20mm/0.78in cannon in Italian aircraft and two 30mm/1.18in cannon in Brazilian) and avionics, the canopy and the tail structure. Embraer is responsible for the air intakes, wings, leading edge slats, flaps, wing pylons and external fuel tanks. Elements are made in both countries and then shipped to the other as each has final assembly facilities. Power is provided by a non-afterburning

Rolls-Royce Spey 807 turbofan built under licence.

The prototype first flew in 1984 and the first AMX aircraft was delivered to the Italian Air Force in January 1989 and to the Brazilian Air Force in 1990. In total, 192 aircraft, 155 single-seaters and 37 AMX-T two-seaters have been delivered to Italy and Brazil. In December 2002, the Venezuelan Air Force signed a contract for 12 AMX-T aircraft.

Although the primary role of the AMX is ground attack, the aircraft is also highly effective in the air defence mission – in fact, so much so that in 1999, Italian Air Force AMXs were deployed as part of the NATO forces in Operation Allied Force against Serbia.

The AMX Advanced Trainer Attack (AMX-ATA) is a new AMX two-seater, multi-mission attack fighter for combat roles and advanced training. AMX-ATA incorporates new sensors, a forward-looking infrared, helmet-mounted display, a new multi-mode radar for anti-air and anti-ship capability, and new

## AMX International AMX

**First flight:** May 15, 1984

**Power:** One licence-built Rolls-Royce 5008kg/ 11,030lb thrust Spey 807 turbofan

**Armament:** One 20mm/0.78in cannon (two 30mm/ 1.18in in Brazilian aircraft); weapons load of up to 3800kg/8364lb comprising bombs, rockets and air-to-air missiles

**Size:** Wingspan – 8.87m/29ft 2in
Length – 13.23m/43ft 5in
Height – 4.55m/14ft 11in
Wing area – 21m²/226.1sq ft

**Weights:** Empty – 6700kg/14,747lb
Maximum take-off – 13,000kg/28,613lb

**Performance:** Maximum speed – 915kph/568mph
Ceiling – 13,008m/42,650ft
Range – 1852km/1150 miles
Climb – 3126m/10,250ft per minute

weapon systems, including anti-ship missiles and medium-range missiles. The Venezuelan Air Force ordered eight AMX-ATAs in 1999 for the advanced trainer and attack aircraft role.

# Avro Lincoln

The Lincoln, originally known as the Lancaster IV, was produced to meet a British Air Ministry requirement for a Lancaster replacement. In 1943, Air Ministry planners were turning their thoughts to developing a long-range bomber force (Tiger Force) for action in the Pacific. These new aircraft had to be able to cover the vast distances between likely take-off points and targets.

Elements of the Lancaster were indeed featured in the new design, and the family resemblance is clear, but the aircraft was a sufficiently different design to be named Lincoln instead. A larger fuselage was carried by a new wing and the aircraft was protected by heavier armament. The increased weight required a stronger undercarriage assembly. The prototype, with Captain Brown at the controls, took to the air for the first time at Ringway, Manchester, on June 9, 1944.

Lancaster production had to remain high, so Lincolns did not reach RAF squadrons until August 1945. World War II ended before the Lincoln made it to the Pacific theatre, but the aircraft equipped post-war Bomber Command in the difficult and tense period before the jet-powered V-Bombers were available.

Lincolns went on to equip around 20 squadrons of RAF Bomber Command but it was soon realized that the Lincoln was somewhat lacking in a world increasingly dominated by jets. This led to partial replacement in RAF service by hastily

TOP: **The Lancaster connection is clear, but there was much that was new about the Lincoln.** ABOVE: **The Lincoln I began to reach RAF units in August 1945.**

acquired ex-USAF B-29s. However, Lincolns did see action against communist terrorists in Malaya in 1950 and Mau-Mau dissidents in Kenya from 1953. Lincolns were finally replaced in the RAF by the V-Bombers from 1955. The last Lincolns in RAF service were used in radar development trials until May 1963.

Australia undertook construction of what was designated the Lincoln Mk 30 at the Government Aircraft Factory (GAF), and the first GAF Lincoln, A73-1, flew in March 1946. The first four were assembled mainly from British parts but the rest were manufactured locally. The GAF Lincolns were powered by both British and Australian engines. A number of special "heavy-lift" aircraft were known as Mk 30As. Twelve aircraft were completed as long-nosed Mk 31s, the nose housing three crew. The Lincoln GR.31 was a unique Australian version developed for anti-submarine work. Royal Australian Air Force Lincolns also took part in the Malayan Emergency.

In the latter stages of World War II, Canada had also ordered home production of the Lincoln to equip Canadian bomber units destined for the Pacific. When war ended, production was stopped after only six aircraft had been started. Post-war, the RCAF evaluated the Lincoln but chose not to produce or buy any more. The only export customer for British-built Lincolns was the Argentine Air Force, which acquired 30 Lincoln Mk IIs in 1947.

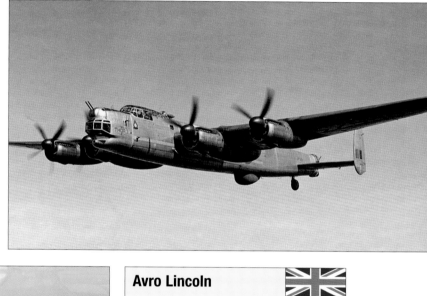

TOP: **The Lincoln II, or B.2 as it was known in service, differed from the Mk I in its engines, which were Merlin 66, 68A or 300s.** RIGHT: **For the tense years after World War II while the new jet bombers were developed, the Lincoln was Bomber Command's main weapon.** BELOW: **RAF Lincolns were used in combat in Malaya and Kenya.**

### Avro Lincoln

**First flight:** June 9, 1944
**Power:** Four Rolls-Royce 1750hp Merlin 85 in-line piston engines
**Armament:** Two 12.7mm/0.5in machine-guns each in turrets in tail, nose and dorsal position; up to 6356kg/14,000lb of bombs
**Size:** Wingspan – 36.58m/120ft
Length – 23.86m/78ft 3.5in
Height – 5.27m/17ft 3.5in
Wing area – 132m²/1421sq ft
**Weights:** Empty – 19,522kg/43,000lb
Maximum take-off – 34,050kg/75,000lb
**Performance:** Maximum speed – 475kph/295mph
Service ceiling – 9302m/30,500ft
Range – 2366km/1470 miles
Climb – 245m/800ft per minute

# Avro Shackleton

During World War II, Britain learned that enemy submarines could wreak havoc with seaborne supply routes in the Atlantic. While surface vessels can be effective against submarines, they can only patrol a relatively small area, and they themselves are at risk from submarines. In contrast, RAF Coastal Command's Lend-Lease Fortresses, Liberators and Catalinas were able to range over vast areas of ocean on a single patrol, and destroyed around 200 German submarines.

Realizing the strategic necessity for effective maritime reconnaissance aircraft in the RAF inventory, and mindful of the fact that Lend-Lease types would be returning to the USA, the Air Ministry issued a 1946 requirement for a British replacement. Avro's design, which became the Shackleton, was selected, possibly because the new aircraft was to employ some elements of the already familiar Avro Lincoln bomber. The Lincoln's wings and undercarriage were mated to a new design fuselage and the aircraft was powered by the higher-performance Griffon engines which turned six-blade contra-rotating propellers. Because of the very long duration of maritime patrol missions, crew comfort was taken seriously, as was soundproofing to protect the ten-man crew against the horrific noise levels generated by four snarling Griffons. Despite the best efforts of the designers, the main wing spar, which passed straight through the fuselage, continued to be a major obstacle when moving from the front to the rear of the aircraft, as had been the case on both the Lincoln and the Lancaster before it.

TOP: **The Shackleton protected Britain's interests on land, sea and in the air for over three decades.** ABOVE: **The Shackleton prototype, VW126, which had its maiden flight on March 9, 1949.**

The first of three Shackleton M.R.1 prototypes, VW126, took to the air on March 9, 1949. The M.R.I and M.R.IA (denoting differing powerplant detail) began to enter RAF service in February 1951. This first Shackleton version is easy to identify thanks to the large "chin" radome, which proved to be problematic as it failed to provide the ideal 360-degree cover and was susceptible to bird-strike. In the Mk 2 Shackleton, which entered RAF service in late 1952, the radar was moved back to the ventral position and was housed in a retractable radome. The nose of this version was also lengthened, and acquired a bomb-aimer's and a nose-gunner's position armed with two 20mm/0.78in Hispano cannons.

When the Shackleton M.R.3 entered service in late 1957, it introduced the tricycle undercarriage, much to the pilots' delight. Crews had voiced concerns over landing the tail-dragger versions because the Shackleton was a heavy aircraft to land with a tailwheel – several tons heavier than

## Avro Shackleton M.R.2

**First flight:** June 17, 1952
**Power:** Four Rolls-Royce 2455hp Griffon 57A V-12
   piston engines
**Armament:** Two pairs of 20mm/0.78in cannon;
   maximum weapons-bay load of 8172kg/
   18,000lb of bombs or depth charges
**Size:** Wingspan – 36.58m/120ft
   Length – 26.59m/87ft 3in
   Height – 5.1m/16ft 9in
   Wing area – 132m²/1421sq ft
**Weights:** Empty –25,379kg/55,900lb
   Maximum take-off – 39,044kg/86,000lb
**Performance:** Maximum speed – 500kph/311mph
   Ceiling – 6405m/21,000ft
   Range – 5440km/3380 miles
   Climb – 260m/850ft per minute

ABOVE: **Normally based at Lossiemouth in Scotland, this Shackleton AEW2 is pictured at Gibraltar.** LEFT: **The AEW2 Shackletons flew on long after their anticipated retirement, while a replacement was finalized.** BELOW: **The MR3 carried extra fuel for its long overwater flights in tip-tanks at the end of the wing.** BOTTOM: **The M.R.3 introduced the tricycle undercarriage, while the mid-upper turret of earlier versions was deleted.**

a Lancaster, for example. The tricycle gear also made taxiing rather less stressful for those on the flightdeck and probably for those on the ground too. More efficient braking, a greater fuel load, full sound insulation (needed on an 18-hour mission), a galley and rest area were all introduced in the Mark 3. It was this version that was exported to South Africa, whose No.35 Squadron operated them until 1984.

As more equipment was carried, the all-up weight rose sharply, so to assist with take-off from shorter runways, two Viper jet engines (similar to those used to power the BAC Strikemaster) were fitted to the outboard engine nacelles from 1966. The stresses caused by the use of this modification ultimately shortened the flying life of the Mk 3 aircraft.

The 1956 Suez crisis marked the Shackleton's "combat" debut, providing anti-submarine cover for the British and French ships below. "Shacks" were frequently involved in colonial policing and saw action in Oman, Kuwait and Borneo, but over the years the type also carried out humanitarian and relief missions in areas affected by natural disasters as far afield as Jamaica, Belize and Morocco. The Shackleton, with its long endurance and ability to carry a great deal of rescue equipment, made it an excellent search-and-rescue (SAR) platform.

However, the Shackleton's principal role was the tracking of potentially hostile vessels on and below the surface of the sea. For hunting submarines the aircraft carried a radar which could detect a submarine's snorkel as it broke the sea surface up to 56km/35 miles away.

From the late 1960s, Shackletons were gradually replaced by Nimrods in the maritime reconnaissance role, but the old Avro aircraft continued to fly into the 1980s, modified to serve in the airborne early warning (AEW) role, guarding mainly the northern approaches to Britain.

# Avro Vulcan

The Vulcan, surely one of the most remarkable-looking aircraft ever built, seemed to owe more to the inhabitants of other planets than the German wartime research which influenced its design. The aircraft was Avro's futuristic and adventurous response to a 1946 Air Ministry Operational Requirement calling for a bomber able to carry a 4540kg/ 10,000lb atomic bomb to a target 2775km/1725 miles away.

The Avro Type 698 was conceived as a high-altitude atomic bomber, and was the first four-engine delta-wing aircraft. The unconventional wing shape was chosen because it combines good load-carrying capabilities and high subsonic speed at altitude. To help gain data for the radical new design, several "mini-Vulcans" research aircraft were built – the Avro Type 707s. Gradually the design was changed before the well-known Vulcan layout was finalized. What had been a flying wing with wingtip fins acquired a single central fin, the nose was extended and a distinct fuselage section evolved.

The prototype VX770 flew in August 1952, piloted by Wing Commander Roly Falk, and in 1953 the type 698 was officially named the Vulcan. Spectacular Farnborough appearances followed, the most amazing being a full roll at the 1955 show.

After a redesign of the wing and the addition of more powerful engines, the Vulcan B.1 entered RAF service in February 1957, and became operational with No.83 Squadron at Waddington in July of the same year. Britain's nuclear

TOP: **VX770, the Vulcan prototype, was powered by 2952kg/6500lb thrust Avon turbojets, a long way from the 9080kg/20,000lb thrust Olympus engines that powered the later B.2.** ABOVE: **Vulcan B.1, pictured with its fellow V-bomber, the Victor.**

deterrent force had to be effective and hard-hitting, and it became clear that the B.1 was increasingly vulnerable to the improved Soviet defences it would have to overcome if it were to strike deep into the Soviet Union. To increase the chances of the RAF crews reaching their objectives, the Vulcan B.2 was proposed, with more powerful engines, an electronic warfare (ECM) suite in an enlarged tailcone, and an inflight refuelling capability, along with an improved, larger wing. Some B.1s had a few B.2 improvements incorporated and were designated B.1As. With a longer range, the ability to carry a heavier bomb load (two nuclear weapons instead of one) and greatly improved self-defence capability, the B.2 ensured that the British nuclear strike force was a very real threat to the Soviet Union.

Even with the new and improved B.2, the delivery of free-fall nuclear weapons into the heart of the Soviet Union was probably still a one-way ticket for Vulcan crews. To improve their survivability, a stand-off nuclear missile – the Blue Steel – was developed, which could be launched 161km/100 miles away from the target. Blue Steels were carried partially recessed in the Vulcan's modified bomb bay.

Due to the improvements in Soviet air defence technology, the Vulcans became increasingly vulnerable at high level over enemy territory. The solution was to bring the Vulcan force down to low level, and the aircraft in service were upgraded to B.2A standard. More powerful Olympus engines were fitted, together with terrain-following radar in the nose and a warning radar atop the fin. The Vulcan's role changed when Royal Navy Polaris-equipped submarines took on responsibility for Britain's strategic nuclear deterrent, and they were switched to a tactical low-level penetration role.

However, it was with conventional weapons that the Vulcan first went to war in 1982, when it was used against Argentine positions on the Falkland Islands in what were then the longest bombing raids in history. Vulcans also served in strategic reconnaissance and air-refuelling tanker roles before being withdrawn from service in 1984 to be replaced by Tornadoes. Avro built 144 Vulcans in total, a small number considering the impact that the design had on the aerospace world, and the affection felt for the "tin triangle" by air-show fans the world over.

ABOVE RIGHT: **The Vulcan B.2 was able to carry two nuclear bombs and had increased survivability compared to earlier Vulcans.** RIGHT: **The Vulcan bomb bay carried extra fuel tanks in later versions, but was originally designed to carry the enormous Blue Danube bomb.** BELOW: **Compare the kinked leading edge wing of this B.2 to the pure delta of the prototype.**

---

### Avro Vulcan B.2A

**First flight:** August 30, 1952 (Avro 698 prototype)

**Power:** Four Rolls-Royce 9080kg/20,000lb thrust Olympus 301 turbojets

**Armament:** Twenty-one 454kg/1000lb bombs, nuclear bombs or one Blue Steel stand-off missile

**Size:** Wingspan – 33.85m/111ft
Length – 30.5m/99ft 11in
Height – 8.26m/7ft 1in
Wing area – 368m²/3964sq ft

**Weights:** Empty – Approximately 37,682kg/83,000lb (Mk 1)
Maximum take-off – 113,500kg/250,000lb

**Performance:** Maximum speed – 1038kph/645mph
Ceiling – 16775m/55,000ft
Range – 5550km/3450 miles
Climb – Not published

# BAC/BAE Strikemaster

The origins of the BAC 167 Strikemaster can be traced back to the piston-powered Hunting/Percival Provost basic trainer which first flew in 1950. Hunting swiftly proposed a jet-powered successor to the Provost – the Jet Provost – as a basic jet trainer for the Royal Air Force. Retaining the wings and tail of the original piston aircraft, the Jet Provost also introduced a tricycle undercarriage. From the mid-1950s, the "JP" was the RAF's standard basic jet trainer until it was finally retired in 1993, having being replaced by the Tucano.

The final production version of the Jet Provost was the Mk. 5 which introduced, among other refinements, a pressurized cabin. Following some exports of the Mk 5, it was this version that the manufacturers BAC (Hunting became part of the British Aircraft Corporation in 1961) developed as a private venture into a dedicated combat aircraft, the Strikemaster, which, as a two-seater, still retained a trainer capability.

The Strikemaster first flew in October 1967, and boasted side-by-side ejection seats and the ability to carry 1362kg/ 3000lb of ordnance on eight underwing hardpoints. Armament included free-fall or retarded bombs, gun packs or napalm. Alternatively, a reconnaissance pod, extra fuel tanks or a gun camera could be carried.

The aircraft's simplicity coupled with exceptionally good manoeuvrability and handling were features of the bomber, which attracted numerous overseas customers. Powered by a Rolls-Royce Viper turbojet, the aircraft was designed for operation from rough and short airstrips.

Customers for this very capable combat aircraft, which appeared in a variety of export versions, included Oman (Mk 82 and 82A), Singapore (Mk 84), Botswana, Ecuador (Mk 89), Kenya (Mk 87), Kuwait (Mk 83), New Zealand (Mk 88), Saudi Arabia (Mk 80 and 80A), Sudan (Mk 55) and South Yemen.

RIGHT: **This Strikemaster is painted in the colours of the Singapore Air Defence Command.** BELOW: **The Royal Saudi Air Force was a major customer for the Strikemaster.**

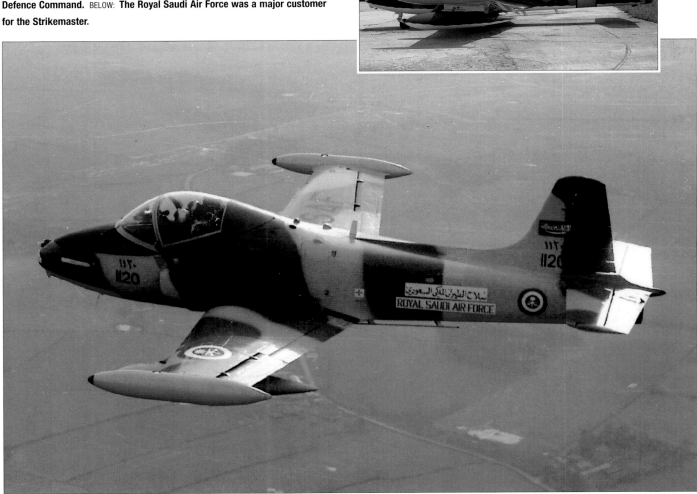

Apart from training, the Strikemaster was most commonly used for ground-attack and counter-insurgency operations. The aircraft of Ecuador, Oman and South Yemen are known to have seen combat – all 20 of the Sultan of Oman's Strikemasters have sustained battle damage.

Between 1968 and 1977, the Royal Saudi Air Force took delivery of a total of 47 Strikemasters in three separate batches. All the aircraft were used for training purposes at the King Faisal Air Academy in Riyadh until 1997, making the Strikemaster one of the longest serving aircraft in RSAF history.

Of the 16 Strikemasters acquired by the Royal New Zealand Air Force (where the aircraft was nicknamed "Blunty") in 1972, use of the aircraft was restricted after 1981 when cracks were discovered in the wing and tail structures of most RNZAF aircraft. The rigours of flying through low-level turbulence and

high usage were given as the likely causes. Replacing the wings of all their aircraft was considered too costly by the RNZAF, who retired them in 1992. Similar problems with the Strikemasters of Ecuador caused the grounding of their fleet for months at a time, while causes were identified and where possible remedied.

The final batch of new Strikemasters was delivered to Sudan in 1984. In all, 146 Strikemasters were sold around the world and many have now been refurbished for civilian use, surviving as "warbirds" in Britain, the USA and Australia.

BELOW LEFT: **In this view of an RNZAF Strikemaster, the side-by-side seats can be clearly seen.** BELOW: **The Strikemaster was one of the first small but capable and affordable trainer/ground-attack aircraft available to smaller nations. There was clearly a demand for this type, and the Strikemaster satisfied that for many nations.**

ABOVE: **An Omani Strikemaster armed with bombs and rockets – the aircraft supplied to Oman saw considerable action.**

## BAC Strikemaster

**First flight:** October 26, 1967
**Power:** One Rolls-Royce 1548kg/3410lb thrust Viper Mk 535 turbojet
**Armament:** Two 7.62mm/0.3in machine-guns; maximum bomb load of 1362kg/3000lb
**Size:** Wingspan – 11.23m/36ft 10in
   Length – 10.27m/33ft 8.5in
   Height – 3.34m/10ft 11.5in
   Wing area – 19.85m²/213.7sq ft
**Weights:** Empty – 2812kg/6195lb
   Maximum take-off – 5221kg/11,500lb
**Performance:** Maximum speed – 760kph/ 472mph
   Ceiling – 12,200m/40,000ft
   Range – 2224km/1382 miles
   Climb – 1601m/5250ft per minute

# British Aircraft Corporation TSR.2

Few British aircraft have stirred as much controversy or strength of feeling as the TSR.2. The project's cancellation in 1965 was seen by many commentators as a political step that became the deathblow for Britain's troubled aviation industry.

The TSR.2 (Tactical Strike and Reconnaissance) was initially designed to meet a demanding 1957 Royal Air Force requirement for a Canberra tactical bomber replacement with terrain-following radar, advanced inertial navigation, supersonic speed at low level and Mach 2 at high altitude. In addition, the new aircraft would ideally have the capability to be operated from short, rough landing strips.

Despite the facts that the requirement become more demanding as development progressed, and that most of the TSR.2's systems were totally new to the British aviation industry, the aircraft began to take shape.

TSR.2's form was of course dictated by the missions it was designed to carry out, but by way of comparison it was longer than an Avro Lancaster but had a smaller wingspan than a Spitfire fighter. The short wingspan was essential for supersonic performance at very low altitude but would fail to generate sufficient lift for it to operate from short strips. The solution was to fit the aircraft with the most powerful blown flaps ever made, which used high-speed air blown over the flaps to make the wing produce massive amounts of lift at take-off and landing.

The TSR.2 carried equipment that is now commonplace but was extremely advanced for the time. A projected moving map, head-up display (HUD), one of the first terrain-following radars and a canopy coated with gold alloy to reflect nuclear

TOP: **XR219, the prototype TSR.2, during its test programme.** ABOVE: **The TSR.2 was equipped with pioneering terrain-following radar, which would have guided the aircraft at heights of 91m/200ft at the speed of sound.**

flash were all cutting-edge features of this remarkable aircraft. The avionics – purpose-designed for the aircraft – would have used forward- and side-looking radar and other systems to feed updated position and steering information to the pilot's HUD, the navigator, the weapon arming and release systems and the autopilot simultaneously. If the whole system had failed, the aircraft would have been automatically put in a climb. Among the materials used in the aircraft's construction were aluminium-copper alloys, aluminium-lithium alloys and ultra-high tensile steel.

The first flight of prototype XR219 took off from Boscombe Down on September 27, 1964, with Roland "Bee" Beamont at the controls and Don Bowen as navigator. The Olympus

## BAC TSR.2

**First flight:** September 27, 1964

**Power:** Two Bristol Siddeley 14982kg/33,000lb thrust Olympus 22R turbojets

**Armament:** Up to 1816kg/4000lb of weapons on underwing pylons; proposed bomb load of up to 2724kg/6000lb

**Size:** Wingspan – 11.28m/37ft
Length – 27.13m/89ft
Height – 7.32m/24ft
Wing area – 65.03m²/700sq ft

**Weights** Empty – 90,000kg/198,090lb
Maximum take-off – 188,000kg/413,788lb

**Performance:** Maximum speed – 2390kph/1485mph
Ceiling – 17,080m/56,000ft
Range – 4827km/3000 miles
Climb – 15,250m/50,000ft per minute
(these figures may not have been achieved in testing but are in the aircraft's specification)

ABOVE LEFT: **XR222, the fourth TSR.2, is preserved at the Imperial War Museum Duxford in the UK.** LEFT: **XR222 prior to its "completion", at least for display purposes, at the Imperial War Museum Duxford.** BELOW LEFT: **During the 24 flights made by XR219, the aircraft's capabilities were clear to the crew.** BELOW: **A rare view of the "hotseat", the pilot's cockpit of TSR.2.**

engines being developed for TSR.2 had some problems (including exploding examples) that had not been resolved before this first flight. The team were keen to get the aircraft into the air as soon as possible in the hope that its remarkable performance would silence the critics. Consequently it was decided that one test-flight could be made with the imperfect engines that were considered likely to explode at more than 97 per cent power. The 14-minute test-flight was uneventful and the aircraft was shown to be responsive and stable.

During further test-flights, the extremely complex aircraft showed that it had the potential to become one of the most formidable strike aircraft in the world. The aircraft made 24 flights and accumulated 13 hours and 9 minutes of flight time, including some at supersonic speeds, before the TSR.2 project was cancelled by the new Labour government on April 6, 1965. The government cited spiralling costs and the minimum 3-year delay in the TSR.2 reaching squadron service as reasons for the decision. The RAF never did receive an alternative to the TSR-2 as a supersonic strike successor to the Canberra.

# BAE Systems Harrier

British innovation in aircraft design is perhaps best demonstrated by the Harrier. This truly remarkable aircraft, constantly improved and updated since its first uncertain hovering flight in October 1960, is still the only single-engined vertical or short take-off and landing (V/STOL) in service.

During the Cold War it was obvious that the West's military airfields would have been attacked very early in any offensive. Dispersal of aircraft and equipment was one option of response – the other was the Harrier, with its ability to operate from any small piece of flat ground. The fact that an aircraft can fly straight up with no need for forward movement still leaves spectators stunned over four decades after the prototype first flew.

The Harrier can take off and land vertically by the pilot selecting an 80-degree nozzle angle and applying full power. At 15–30m/50–100ft altitude, the nozzles are gradually directed rearwards until conventional wingborne flight is achieved. The key to the Harrier's vertical take-off lies with the vectored thrust from the Harrier's Pegasus engine, directed by four jet nozzles controlled by a selector lever next to the throttle in the cockpit. The nozzles swivel as one, directing thrust from directly to the rear to just forward of vertical. While hovering or flying at very low speeds, the aircraft is controlled in all lanes of movement by reaction control jets located in the nose, wing and tail. These jets are operated by the Harrier's conventional rudder pedals and control column.

The Harrier GR1 first entered squadron service with the RAF in October 1969, and many were subsequently upgraded to GR3 standard, with more powerful engines and a tail warning radar to alert the pilot to hostile missiles locking on

TOP: **An RAF GR7. The Harrier is one of the all-time great combat aircraft. The basic soundness of the concept has lent itself to many upgrades and improvements.** ABOVE: **Radar-equipped AV-8Bs of the Spanish Navy operating from the carrier *Principe de Asturias*. These aircraft were similar to those operated by the Italian Navy and USMC aircraft.**

to his aircraft. GR3s of No.1 Squadron RAF were in action during the 1982 Falklands War. They carried out ground-attack operations using cluster and "smart" bombs, with weapon loads of up to 1362kg/3000lb. The Squadron flew more than 150 missions, with two aircraft lost to heavy anti-aircraft fire at Goose Green.

Early in the Harrier's operational life, the US Marine Corps expressed an interest in the aircraft, leading to more than a hundred being built as the AV-8A by McDonnell Douglas in the USA. The USMC continues to operate Harriers today, the AV-8B variant being roughly equivalent to the RAF's GR7. US Marine Corps AV-8Bs took part in Operation Desert Storm in 1991. The other customer for the early Harrier was the Spanish Navy, which ordered the US-built AV-8A, and subsequently sold some of the aircraft on to the Thai Navy in 1996.

ABOVE: **The GR7 is the RAF equivalent of the American-designed AV-8B.**
LEFT: **The Harrier gives its operators unparalled strike flexibility.**

The second-generation GR5 and GR7 versions replaced the original Harrier GR3s in the late 1980s/early 1990s in the offensive support role. The GR7 is, in essence, a licence-built American-designed AV-8B Harrier II fitted with RAF-specific navigation and defensive systems as well as other changes, including additional underwing pylons for Sidewinder missiles. The improved design of the GR7 allows the aircraft to carry twice the load of a GR3 over the same distance or the same load over twice the distance. The first flight of the Harrier GR7 was in 1989, and deliveries to RAF squadrons began in 1990. A total of 96 aircraft were ordered, including 62 interim GR5s which were later modified to GR7 standard.

The Harrier GR7 is capable of operating throughout the full spectrum of ground-attack operations by day and night. The aircraft carries forward-looking infrared (FLIR) equipment which, when used in conjunction with the pilot's night-vision goggles (NVGs), provides a night, low-level capability. The Harrier T10, a two-seat trainer version of the GR7, came into service in 1995 and can be used operationally.

Recent operational deployments for the Harriers have been to Italy in support of NATO and UN operations in Bosnia and Serbia, and to the Gulf embarked on Royal Navy aircraft carriers, where they complemented the Royal Navy's own Sea Harriers.

Plans in 2002 announced the withdrawal of the Sea Harrier by 2006, with the Harrier GR7/GR9s being operated by both RAF and Royal Navy squadrons.

The Harrier continues to be upgraded. New Pegasus 107 engines, giving more thrust at higher temperatures, make the aircraft Harrier GR7As even more efficient. Also, a major upgrade to the aircraft's avionics and weapons systems will enable the Harrier to carry a variety of current and future weapons. These include Maverick air-to-surface missiles, Brimstone anti-armour missiles and Sidewinder air-to-air missiles for self-defence. A new, stronger composite rear fuselage will also be fitted. These aircraft will become Harrier GR9s, while those with the uprated engines and weapons systems will be Harrier GR9As. The programme also includes an upgrade of the two-seater T10 aircraft to the equivalent GR9 standard known as the Harrier T12.

RAF Harriers saw service in Kosovo and in the 2003 invasion of Iraq. On March 22, 2003, alongside aircraft of the USAF and USN, the RAF were heavily involved in attacks against key Iraqi targets, including Baghdad. One of the RAF raids featured the first operational use of the RAF's Maverick missile. A Harrier GR7 pilot launched one of the missiles against a mobile SCUD missile launch site some 322km/200 miles into Iraq. It successfully engaged and destroyed the target.

ABOVE: **The Harrier GR7 can carry up to 4903kg/10,800lb of ordnance under its wings and fuselage.**

### BAE Systems Harrier II GR7

**First flight:** October 21, 1960 (P1127)
**Power:** One Rolls-Royce 9765kg/21,500lb thrust Pegasus Mk5 turbofan
**Armament:** Two 25mm/0.90in cannon; up to 4903kg/10,800lb bombs, missiles or rockets
**Size:** Wingspan – 9.25m/30ft 4in
    Length – 14.36m/47ft 1in
    Height – 3.55m/11ft 7.75in
    Wing area – 21.37m²/230sq ft
**Weights:** Empty – 6973kg/15,360lb
    Maximum take-off – 14,074kg/31,000lb
**Performance:** Maximum speed – 1058kph/661mph
    Ceiling – 15,250m/50,000ft plus
    Range – 11,861km/7370 miles
    Climb – Not available

# Blackburn Buccaneer

The Buccaneer was at one point the most advanced high-speed low-level strike aircraft in the world. It had its origins in the July 1953 Naval Staff Requirement NA.39 which called for a long-range carrier-borne strike aircraft capable of carrying a nuclear weapon beneath enemy radar cover and attacking enemy shipping or ports.

Blackburn's N.A.39 design, the B-103, was the successful contender and the development contract was awarded in 1955 – the first of 20 pre-production aircraft took to the air on April 30, 1958, and also appeared at that year's Farnborough air show. The B-103 prototype was powered by 3178kg/7000lb thrust Gyron turbojets, not the much more powerful Spey of later models. The carrier aircraft elements of the design, such as folding wings, folding nose catapult fittings and arrestor hook, were introduced from the fourth aircraft onwards. The aerodynamically advanced aircraft incorporated many innovations, including a rotary bomb-bay door (intended to avoid the drag of conventional bomb-bay doors and weapons carried beneath the aircraft) and a split tail cone which opened to act as airbrakes. The aircraft also had a cutting-edge boundary layer control system in which air from the engines was forced through slits on the wings' leading edges, producing much more lift than that wing would normally give. Increasing the wings' efficiency meant the aircraft could land at lower speed and carry more ordnance.

The miniature detonating cord (MDC), which shatters the cockpit canopy prior to ejection, is now standard on most British fast jets, and was pioneered on the Blackburn design. It was actually developed to aid escape in the event of underwater ejection.

TOP: **Buccaneer S.1 XK534 from the Fleet Air Arm Trials Unit at Lossiemouth. Painted overall in anti-flash white, this was the 18th pre-production aircraft.** ABOVE: **The Buccaneer's wings are able to fold up through 120 degrees from a hinge.**

Royal Navy carrier trials began in January 1960 and the first B-103 deck landing took place on HMS *Victorious* on the 19th of the month. Having given the aircraft the name Buccaneer in 1960, the Navy took delivery of the first production version, the S.1, in July 1962. HMS *Ark Royal* sailed with the first operational Buccaneer squadron, No.801, and its anti-flash white Buccaneers only six months later in January 1963. The Cold War was at one of its chilliest phases and Britain wanted nuclear-capable aircraft in service as soon as possible.

The S.1 was soon shown to be under-powered, and in some conditions the Gyrons could barely lift a loaded Buccaneer off the deck within safety margins. Consequently, Fleet Air Arm Scimitars fitted with inflight refuelling equipment were detailed to refuel the partly fuelled and therefore lighter Buccaneers shortly after they left the deck. Forty S.1s were built before production switched to the next Mark. The improved S.2 was the principal production version (84 were built) and had a greater range than the earlier version thanks to the more powerful but less thirsty Spey engines. Service S.2s are most easily recognized by the fixed refuelling probe forward of the cockpit.

The S.2s served in the Royal Navy's front line from January 1967 until the last S.2s left the deck of the *Ark Royal* in November 1978. However, the Buccaneer's career was far from over as the first of almost 90 aircraft had begun service with the Royal Air Force in October 1969, filling the gap in the RAF inventory left by the scrapping of TSR.2 and the cancellation of the intended F-111 purchase for the RAF. Twenty-six of the aircraft were new-build while a further 62 Royal Navy examples were gradually transferred into RAF service. In addition to retaining a nuclear strike capability, Buccaneers were also tasked with anti-shipping missions from land bases. RAF Germany, right in the nuclear front-line, first welcomed No.15 Squadrons Buccaneers early in 1971. Tornados began to replace the Germany Buccaneers in 1983 but two squadrons tasked with maritime strike remained in service in Scotland. In 1991 some of these aircraft were "called up" for service in the first Gulf War, where they acted as laser designators for laser-guided bombs dropped by Tornados. To give it an even longer range for these special missions, the "Bucc" was fitted with a 2000 litre/440 gallon fuel tank carried in the bomb bay.

TOP RIGHT: **Buccaneers served on Royal Navy carriers from 1962 until 1978.**
MIDDLE RIGHT: **Some Royal Navy aircraft were transferred to the RAF, while others were brand new aircraft. Some of these retained a nuclear strike capability based in Germany.** RIGHT: **The last Buccaneers in RAF service were those retained for the maritime strike role.** BELOW: **The last British bomber was tasked with demanding Gulf War missions shortly before its retirement.**

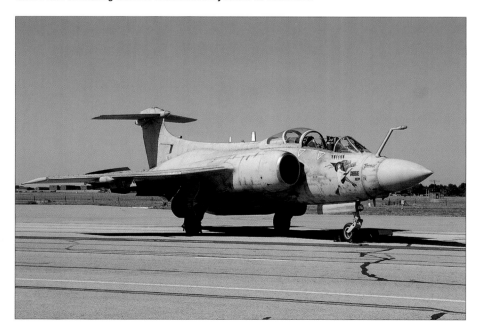

## Blackburn Buccaneer S.2

**First flight:** April 30, 1958 (B-103 prototype)
**Power:** Two Rolls-Royce 5039kg/11,100lb thrust Rolls-Royce Spey 101 turbofans
**Armament:** One nuclear bomb or four 454kg/1000lb conventional bombs carried internally
**Size:** Wingspan – 13.41m/44ft
Length – 19.33m/63ft 5in
Height – 4.95m/16ft 3in
Wing area – 47.82m²/514.7sq ft
**Weights:** Empty –13,620kg/30,000lb
Maximum takeoff – 28,148kg/62,000lb
**Performance:** Maximum speed – 1038kph/645mph
Ceiling – 12,200m/40,000ft plus
Range – 3218km/2000 miles
Climb – 9150m/30,000ft in 2 minutes

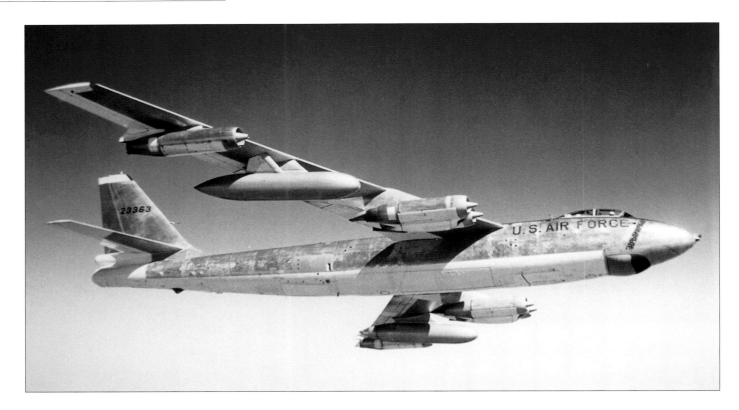

# Boeing B-47 Stratojet

As World War II was drawing to a close, the US Army Air Forces were considering replacements for the aircraft types then in service. Development of a new subsonic, high-altitude, medium-range bomber began in 1945 with four US contractors in the running. The Boeing design, the six-jet XB-47 (first flight December 1947), with the performance of contemporary jet fighters, won the competition and became the first jet-powered swept-wing bomber in service. Its six turbojet engines (so many were needed because of the poor power output of early jets) were housed in pods slung beneath the 35-degree swept-back wings, the inboard pods housing two engines each while a single engine was positioned towards the tip of each wing. Early versions at maximum take-off weight needed additional thrust from 18 solid-fuel booster rockets in the aft fuselage.

B-47s began entering the USAF inventory in 1952 and, in the days before intercontinental ballistic missiles, the fast nuclear-armed bomber was the best deterrent the USA had. Apart from the swept wings and profusion of engines, the aircraft incorporated many novel features, including a remote-controlled tail gun turret and a bicycle-type retractable main landing gear with single, two-wheel legs on the forward and aft fuselage. Outrigger wheels that retracted into the two-engine pod cowling provided added stability. The B-model was the first production version in service but was supplanted by the B-47E, the ultimate bomber version.

The three-man B-47 was a heavy aircraft in its day, and although it was a medium-range bomber, it was heavier than any strategic bomber aircraft of World War II. A tail chute was used to slow down the aircraft during landings, one of the first aircraft to use the technique. The B-47 could carry a 9080kg/ 20,000lb bomb load that limited the aircraft to a maximum of two nuclear weapons of the early 1950s. However, so many B-47s were manufactured, they did represent a more than credible deterrent or threat to the Soviet Union. Conventional weaponry options included 6129kg/13,500lb or eight 454kg/ 1000lb bombs.

The B-47 had a 5792km/3600 mile range which required Strategic Air Command to make use of forward bases in friendly nations such as Britain, Spain and Morocco, as well as

ABOVE: **The B-47 was a great technological leap for US military aviation. The main bomber at the time of the B-47's first flight was the B-29.** LEFT: **At its peak use, the B-47 equipped 28 SAC Bomb Wings, each with 45 aircraft.**

LEFT: **The large swept wings, 1-2-2-1 engine layout and the fighter style canopy make the B-47 one of the easiest aircraft to identify.** BELOW: **An early B-47 assisted by 18 rockets at take-off.** BOTTOM: **Over 2000 B-47s were built, and they provided the USA with a credible nuclear deterrent.**

Alaska, to be within striking distance of the USSR. In addition, the B-47 was later equipped with an air-refuelling capability and 36-hour missions were flown to show the world the reach of the SAC bomber. However, when some foreign hosts chose to withdraw their offer of forward bases, the usefulness of the B-47 was reduced because there was insufficient tanker support to allow great numbers of B-47s to operate from the continental USA.

Also, as with Britain's V-force, the B-47 role was changed in the mid-1950s due to the development of effective Soviet surface-to-air missiles (SAMs), and the aircraft's structure was strengthened so that it could be used as a low-level bomber avoiding Soviet radars.

Some B-47s were modified for reconnaissance use (RB-47) and, as space was at a premium in the airframe, these versions were not capable of carrying bombs as well as reconnaissance equipment. However, the RB-47B could be converted back to bomber configuration.

By 1956, B-47 deployment peaked, with over 1300 equipping 28 SAC wings, while around 250 RB-47s were in SAC service in the same period. The B-47 was gradually

phased out in the early 1960s. About 400 were in service in 1964 and by 1966 the last B-47 had been phased out. The retirement of the B-47 was balanced by the large numbers of strategic nuclear missiles then joining the US arsenal. A total of 2039 B-47s were built.

## Boeing B-47E Stratojet

**First flight:** December 17, 1947
**Power:** Six General Electric 3269kg/7200lb thrust J47-GE-25 turbojets
**Armament:** Two 20mm/0.78in cannon in remote-controlled tail turret; up to 9080kg/20,000lb of bombs
**Size:** Wingspan – 35.36m/116ft
Length – 33.48m/109ft 10in
Height – 8.51m/27ft 11in
Wing area –132.66m²/1428sq ft
**Weights:** Empty – 36,663kg/80,756lb
Maximum take-off – 89,973kg/198,180lb
**Peformance:** Maximum speed – 975kph/606mph
Ceiling –12,352m/40,500ft plus
Range – 5794km/3600 miles
Climb – 1326m/4350ft per minute at maximum power

# Boeing B-52 Stratofortress

The B-52 is surely one of the greatest combat aircraft of all time, remaining in front-line service almost six decades after the USAF specification for what became the B-52 was released in 1946. The USAF wanted a bomber with a 16,090km/10,000-mile range and a speed of over 804kph/500mph. Boeing initially proposed a conventional design with piston engines to achieve the range. As the US Air Force wanted the aircraft to fly as high and fast as possible to drop atomic weapons, Boeing revised the design with eight jet powerplants and swept wings.

The prototype first flew in 1952 and ever since entering service in 1955, the B-52 has been in the front line. The first operational version was the B-52B, and in 1956 a B-model dropped the first air-dropped hydrogen bomb over Bikini Atoll. In an attempt to demonstrate the reach of the USAF Strategic Air Command, three B-52Bs made a non-stop flight around the world in January 1957, with the help of five inflight refuellings.

A total of 744 B-52s were built with the last, a B-52H, delivered in October 1962. Only the H-model is still in the Air Force inventory and is assigned to Air Combat Command and the Air Force Reserves. The first of 102 B-52s was delivered to Strategic Air Command in May 1961.

The B-52 could bomb the Soviet Union from bases in the continental USA and was a key element in SAC's deterrence of the Soviet Union. To ensure the survivability of the SAC deterrent against a pre-emptive Soviet strike, the SAC B-52 force was dispersed and rotated. In addition, a given number

TOP: **A B-52D. The B-52 is a truly great military aircraft. Despite being in service for half a century, there is still no other aircraft in the US inventory that can do the job of the B-52, and on the same scale.** ABOVE: **The bomb-carrying capacity of the "Buff" is considerable – 27,240kg/60,000lb of weaponry can be trucked and dropped on a target.**

of B-52s was kept on standby ready for take-off and, for a time, in the air ready to begin attacks on Soviet targets. From 1958 until 1968, ten to twelve USAF B-52s were airborne at all times. At the time of the 1962 Cuban missile crisis, 70 aircraft were kept aloft at all times for one month. Following two crashes in which radioactivity was released from the nuclear bombs aboard, the airborne alert ceased.

The B-52, with its cavernous bomb bay and great lifting capability, has been armed with free-fall hydrogen bombs and parachute retarded bombs as well as stand-off nuclear

LEFT: **The B-52G was a complete structural redesign with a distinctive short fin.** BELOW: **The H-model is the version still in USAF use today, and will be for some years to come.** BOTTOM: **Inflight refuelling during the Gulf War. The conflict gave the old but potent bomber the opportunity to get into the record books with the longest bombing mission in history.**

missiles, including the AGM-86B. Of course, the aircraft has never used nuclear weapons in anger. During the Vietnam War, however, USAF B-52s dropped almost 3 million tons of bombs. The bomb bay of the D-model was modified so that it could carry up to 108 conventional bombs, which meant that each aircraft could carry around 27.4 tonnes/27 tons per aircraft.

Two decades after its missions over Vietnam, the B-52 took part in the Gulf War. Seven B-52s armed with AGM-86 cruise missiles flew 22,500km/14,000 miles (and into the history books) from the USA to carry out the first air strike of the war – this was the longest combat mission ever flown. During the conflict, 80 B-52s flew 1624 sorties, dropping 26,111 tonnes/ 25,700 tons of bombs, accounting for 40 per cent of the total dropped during the war. In 2003, USAF B-52s operating from a base in Britain carried out numerous bombing raids on targets in Iraq, demonstrating that the '52 was still a potent front-line combat aircraft 51 years after the type first flew.

Today, the B-52s of USAF Air Combat Command remain a key means of delivering US air power with worldwide precision navigation capability. The aircraft is also highly effective when used for ocean surveillance, and can assist the US Navy in anti-ship and mine-laying operations. In two hours, two B-52s can monitor 362,600km²/140,000sq miles of ocean surface.

The B-52 is capable of dropping or launching the widest array of weapons in the US inventory. This includes gravity bombs, cluster bombs, precision-guided missiles and joint direct attack munitions. Updated with modern technology, the B-52 will be capable of delivering the full complement of joint developed weapons – current engineering analysis shows the B-52's life span to extend beyond the year 2045. The B-52 will be kept flying because there is nothing else in the US inventory that can carry out the B-52 mission on the same scale.

## Boeing B-52D

**First Flight:** April 15, 1952
**Power:** Eight Pratt & Whitney 5493kg/12,100lb thrust J57-P-19W turbojets
**Armament:** Four 12.7mm/0.5in machine-guns in tail; maximum of 108 conventional bombs up to 27,240kg/60,000lb
**Size:** Wingspan – 56.4m/185ft
Length – 47.7m/156ft 6in
Height – 12.75m/48ft 3.7in
Wing area – 371.6m²/4000sq ft
**Weights:** Empty – 85,806kg/189,000lb
Maximum take-off – 204,300kg/450,000lb
**Performance:** Maximum speed – 893kph/555mph
Ceiling – 13,725m/45,000ft
Range – 11,861km/7370 miles
Climb – Not available

# Boeing/McDonnell Douglas/Northrop F/A-18 Hornet

With its excellent fighter and self-defence capabilities, the F/A-18 was intended to increase strike mission survivability and supplement the F-14 Tomcat in US Navy fleet air defence. The F/A-18 played a key role in the 1986 US strikes against Libya. Flying from the USS *Coral Sea*, F/A-18s launched high-speed anti-radiation missiles (HARMs) against Libyan air-defence radars and missile sites, thus silencing them during the attacks on military targets in Benghazi.

The F/A-18's advanced radar and avionics systems allow Hornet pilots to shift from fighter to strike mode on the same mission with the flip of a switch, a facility used routinely by Hornets in Operation Desert Storm – they fought their way to a target by defeating opposing aircraft, attacked ground targets and returned home safely. This "force multiplier" capability gives the operational commander more flexibility in employing tactical aircraft in a rapidly changing battle scenario.

The F/A-18 Hornet was built in single and two-seat versions. Although the two-seater is a conversion trainer, it is combat-capable and has a similar performance to the single seat version, although with reduced range. The F/A-18A and C are single-seat aircraft, while the F/A-18B and D are dual-seaters. The B-model is used primarily for training, while the D-model is the current Navy aircraft for attack, tactical air control, forward air control and reconnaissance squadrons.

In November 1989, the first F/A-18s equipped with night-strike capability were delivered, and since 1991, F/A-18s have been delivered with F404-GE-402 enhanced performance engines that produce up to 20 per cent more thrust than the previous F404 engines. From May 1994, the Hornet has been equipped with upgraded radar – the APG-73 – which substantially increases the speed and memory capacity of the radar's processors. These upgrades and improvements help the Hornet maintain its advantage over potential enemies and keep it among the most advanced and capable combat aircraft in the world.

Apart from the US Navy and Marine Corps, the F/A-18 is also in service with the air forces of Canada, Australia, Spain, Kuwait, Finland, Switzerland and Malaysia.

Canada was the first international customer for the F/A-18, and its fleet of 138 CF-18 Hornets is the largest outside the USA. The CF-18s have an unusual element to their paint scheme in that a "fake" cockpit is painted on the underside of the fuselage directly beneath the real cockpit. This is intended to confuse an enemy fighter, if only for a split second, about the orientation of the CF-18 in close air combat. That moment's hesitation can mean the difference between kill or be killed in a dogfight situation.

TOP: **The Hornet/Super Hornet family of aircraft have given their operators an exceptional combination of capabilities – few aircraft can fight, not just evade, enemy aircraft and then carry out devastating pinpoint attacks.** ABOVE: **Aircraft operated by Spain were designated EF/A-18. This is a single-seat A-model.**

The F/A-18E/F Super Hornet was devised to build on the great success of the Hornet, and having been test-flown in November 1995, entered service for evaluation with US Navy squadron VFA-122 in November 1999.

The Super Hornet is 25 per cent larger than its predecessor but has 42 per cent fewer parts. Both the single-seat E and two-seat F-models offer increased range, greater endurance, more payload-carrying ability and more powerful engines in the form of the F414-GE-400, an advanced derivative of the Hornet's current F404 engine family that produces 35 per cent more thrust.

Structural changes to the airframe increase internal fuel capacity by 1634kg/3600lb, which extends the Hornet's mission radius by up to 40 per cent. The fuselage is 86.3cm/34in longer and the wing is 25 per cent larger with an extra 9.3m²/100sq ft of surface area. There are two additional weapons stations, bringing the total to 11.

In the words of its manufacturers, "The Super Hornet is an adverse-weather, day and night, multi-mission strike fighter whose survivability improvements over its predecessors make it harder to find, and if found, harder to hit, and if hit, harder to disable."

The first operational cruise of the F/A-18 E Super Hornet was with VFA-115 on board the USS *Abraham Lincoln* on July 24, 2002, and the type was first used in combat on November 6, 2002, when they participated in a strike against hostile targets in the "no-fly" zone in Iraq.

ABOVE: **A US Marine Corps F/A-18D drops a bomb over a bombing range in Nevada.** BELOW LEFT: **A fine air-to-air study of USMC Hornets.** BELOW: **USMC Hornets. The type is operated by a number of other nations outside the USA, on four different continents.** BOTTOM: **The Super Hornet is bigger and better than the original design.**

## Northrop F/A-18E Super Hornet

**First flight:** November 18, 1995
**Power:** Two General Electric 9988kg/22,000lb thrust afterburning F414-GE-400 turbofans
**Armament:** One 20mm/0.78in cannon, eleven hardpoints carrying up to 8058kg/17,750lb of weapons, including AIM-7, AIM-120 AMRAAM, AIM-9 air-to-air missiles or other guided weapons, bombs and rockets
**Size:** Wingspan – 13.62m/44ft 9in
    Length – 18.31m/60ft 1in
    Height – 4.88m/16ft
    Wing area – 46.5m²/500sq ft
**Weights:** Empty – 13,426kg/29,574lb
    Maximum take-off – 29,937kg/66,000lb
**Performance:** Maximum speed – 1915kph/1189mph
    Ceiling – 15,250m/50,000ft plus
    Combat radius – 2225km/1382 miles
    Climb – Not published

# Breguet Alizé

## Breguet Alizé

**First Flight:** March 26, 1955 (prototype)
**Power:** One Rolls-Royce 1975hp DartRDa21 turboprop
**Armament:** Two anti-shipping missiles carried beneath the folding wings, or a combination of depth charges, bombs or rockets; acoustic torpedo, three 160kg/352lb depth charges housed in internal bomb bay
**Size:** Wingspan – 15.6m/51ft 2in
Length – 13.86m/45ft 6in
Height – 5.00m/16ft 4.75in
Wing area – 36.00m²/387.51sq ft
**Weights:** Empty – 5700kg/12,546lb
Maximum take-off – 8200kg/18,048lb
**Performance:** Maximum speed – 518kph/322mph
Ceiling – 8000m/26,245ft plus
Range – 2500km/1553 miles
Climb – 420m/1380ft per minute

ABOVE: **Alizé prepares to take off from a French carrier.** LEFT: **This French Navy Alizé's retractable radome is seen in the stowed position beneath the roundel.** BELOW: **Sporting a French Navy 1990s low-visibility paint scheme.**

The carrier-borne anti-submarine Alizé (tradewind) was derived from the Vultur carrier-based attack aircraft designed for the French Aeronavale but never produced for service. The Alizé was an extensive redesign of the earlier type and had its first flight on October 5, 1956.

The crew of three consisted of pilot, radar operator and sensor operator. The pilot was seated in front to the right, the radar operator in front to the left, and the sensor operator sat sideways behind them. Landing gear retracted backwards into nacelles in the wings. The Alizé, powered by the Rolls-Royce Dart RDa.21 turboprop driving a four-bladed propeller, could patrol for over 5 hours.

The aircraft was armed with a potent array of torpedoes, depth charges, bombs, rockets and missiles. A total of 89 examples of the Alizé were built between 1957 and 1962, including

prototypes. The Aeronavale operated 75 from March 1959 on board the carriers *Clemenceau* and *Foch*.

The Aeronavale upgraded the Alizé in the 1980s and '90s with the latest avionics. The aircraft was simply not able to hunt modern nuclear-powered submarines effectively, so was limited to maritime surface patrol duties.

The Aeronavale operated 24 examples until 1997, and in the spring of 1999, aircraft flying off the carrier

*Foch* were used operationally during the NATO air campaign against Serbia over Kosovo. The Alizé was finally withdrawn from Aeronavale service in 2000 with the retirement of the *Foch*.

The Indian Navy operated the Alizé (at least 12 examples) from shore bases and from the light carrier *Vikrant*. The type was used for reconnaissance and patrol during India's 1961 occupation of Portuguese Goa, and was also used for anti-submarine patrol during the Indo-Pakistan War of 1971. During this conflict, one Alizé was shot down by a Pakistani F-104 Starfighter in what must have been a most unusual air-combat episode. The Alizé was gradually relegated to shore-based patrol duties in the 1980s, and was finally phased out in 1991, replaced by ASW helicopters.

LEFT: **The German Navy have operated Atlantics since the mid-1960s.**
BELOW: **The improved Atlantique 2.**

# Breguet/Dassault Atlantic

In 1956, NATO began to consider a maritime patrol aircraft capable of hunting Soviet nuclear submarines, to replace the ageing Lockheed Neptune. Fourteen countries took part in studies to produce an aircraft that could fly for 18 hours at 300 knots and carry all the equipment and ordnance needed to search for and destroy Soviet submarines. Out of the 25 put forward, Breguet (now Dassault Aviation) proposed the Atlantic, which was ultimately ordered by France (40 aircraft), Germany (20), and later by the Netherlands (9) and Italy (18). Construction was carried out by a consortium of manufacturers across the four nations.

The first Atlantics were delivered to the French Navy in October 1965 and equipped four squadrons who operated them in the maritime reconnaissance role. However, the French aircraft were also used for land reconnaissance over Mauritania and Chad, and during the first Gulf War.

As well as advanced optical equipment, the Atlantic was fitted with highly advanced avionics systems – largely British and American – including a Thomson underfuselage radar able to locate submarines on the surface. Other equipment included a magnetic anomaly detector (MAD) to sense the magnetic fields generated by the metal mass of submerged submarines.

The aircraft could also drop acoustic buoys in a search area which, with the equipment on board, would form a submarine acoustic detection network in which a vessel could be easily located. Having identified a target, the Atlantic could then use a variety of equipment to attack, including bombs, depth charges, homing or acoustic torpedoes, plus a variety of missiles armed with conventional or nuclear warheads.

The French Navy were so impressed by the capability of the Atlantic that they ordered the much-improved Atlantique Mark 2, 28 examples of which were finally delivered between 1989 and 1997.

One of the radars carried on the Mark 2 is so sensitive it can detect a submarine periscope above the surface. The Mark 2's acoustic detection system uses buoys that can not only locate submarines, but will also compare the findings with its database to identify the class, nationality and threat level of the "bogey".

In the event of an enemy attack, the aircraft also has electronic counter-measures to deceive infrared and radar homing missiles. The Atlantique 2 can carry eight torpedoes or two Exocet missiles, or eight pods containing a raft and survival equipment for any survivors of a sinking.

A fully up-to-date glass cockpit Atlantique Mark 3 will be entering French Navy service in 2007, while Germany and Italy hope to replace their original Mark Is with 3s by 2010.

ABOVE: **A view inside the Atlantique 2, which is equipped with the very latest electronic surveillance and processing equipment.**

## Breguet/Dassault Atlantic

**First flight:** October 21, 1961
**Power:** Two Rolls-Royce 6106eshp Tyne 21 turboprops
**Armament:** Up to 6000kg/13,206lb of bombs, depth charges, torpedoes, mines and missiles carried in weapons bay or on underwing pylons
**Size:** Wingspan – 37.42m/122ft 9in
    Length – 33.63m/110ft 4in
    Height – 11.35m/37ft 3in
    Wing area – 120.34m²/1295sq ft
**Weights:** Empty – 25,300kg/55,685lb
    Maximum take-off – 46,200kg/101,686lb
**Performance:** Maximum speed – 6481kph/403mph
    Ceiling – 9150m/30,020ft
    Range – 9075km/5635 miles
    Climb – 746m/2450m per minute

# Convair B-36 Peacemaker

The Convair B-36 Peacemaker was physically the largest bomber to ever have gone into service with the United States Air Force, and during the late 1940s and early '50s, it was the USAF's long-range strategic bombing deterrent. Although it never saw combat, reconnaissance versions flew near or possibly over the Soviet during the height of the Cold War in the mid-1950s.

The B-36 was conceived in the early years of World War II, when the US feared that its ally Britain may have been invaded by Germany. The USA knew that if it was drawn into the war in Europe it would need a means of carrying out attacks from the continental USA. In search of an aircraft capable of carrying out bombing raids over unprecedented distances, on April 11, 1941 the US Army Air Corps invited designs for a bomber with a 724kph/450mph top speed, a cruising speed of 442kph/275mph, a ceiling of 13,725m/45,000ft and a maximum range of 19,308km/12,000 miles. Consolidated's design, the Model 35, had twin fins and rudders, and four or six engines were suggested. To speed up the intercontinental bomber project, the requirements were scaled down to a 16,090km/10,000-mile range, cruising speed of between 386–483kph/240–300mph, and a service ceiling of 12,200m/40,000ft.

In late 1941, Consolidated (later Convair) was asked to proceed to prototype stage (two aircraft) using six engines, and the aircraft was designated XB-36. The aircraft proposed by Consolidated was staggering in its proportions. The slightly swept-back wing spanned 70.1m/230ft with a wing area of 443.32m²/4772sq ft. At that stage the aircraft was powered by six 28-cylinder Pratt & Whitney R-4360 Wasp Major air-cooled radials, each driving a 5.8m/19ft three-bladed Curtiss propeller, unusually, in pusher configuration. These engines were accessible in flight through the truly enormous 2.29m/7.5ft thick wing root. The four bomb bays could carry 20,884kg/46,000lb of bombs, compared to the 9080kg/20,000lb of bombs of the B-29. The fuselage of the aircraft was 49.4m/162ft long, and the crew moved from front to rear through a 0.64m/25in diameter, 24.4m/80ft pressurized tunnel using a wheeled trolley.

In early 1943, the USA faced losing its bases in China to the invading Japanese, so the mighty Convair bomber, with its planned global reach, became an even more important project. Therefore, a June 1943 order was placed for 100 examples of the huge bomber, with the prototype to be ready by September 1944 and service deliveries within a year. Development delays with the engines, among other aspects of the project, almost doomed the aircraft, then Allied progress in the Pacific war reduced the project's priority status. Even when Germany surrendered, the B-36 project stayed alive because the USA needed a means of delivering their atom bomb against potential enemies around the world.

The prototype finally flew, almost two years late, on August 8, 1946. At the time, there were only three runways in the USA strong enough to take the weight of the behemoth bomber, which was the heaviest and largest land-based aircraft to have flown.

BELOW: **Instead of the normal bare-metal finish, this B-36B carries so-called "Arctic red" test markings. The aircraft was operated by the 7th Bomb Group.**

Strategic Air Command ultimately had ten wings equipped with B-36 Peacemakers. A-models were unarmed and used as training aircraft, whereas the B-36B was a nuclear bomber.

As more equipment and fuel increased the weight of the aircraft, the piston engines – developed to produce all the power they could – were augmented by four 2452kg/5400lb thrust turbojets, leading to the "six turning, four burning" description of the B-36's later powerplant arrangements. This model, produced as the B-36D, was complemented by 64 B-models converted to D standard. This ten-engined version was the template for later, more powerful and better-equipped bomber versions.

When production ended in August 1954, 383 aircraft had been built for the USAF. From 1958, the B-36 was replaced in Strategic Air Command by the Boeing B-52. In the ten or so years that the B-36 was in front-line service, it gave the USA a global reach, leaving potential enemies in no doubt that they could be attacked by America. If one accepts that deterrence kept the peace at this time in the Cold War, then the B-36 could indeed have no better name than "Peacemaker".

ABOVE: **The B-36D, "six turning and four burning".**
LEFT: **The RB-36D was a reconnaissance version of Convair's "Big Stick" – the endurance and carrying power of the aircraft allowed it to undertake strategic reconnaissance missions.** BELOW LEFT: **The scale of the B-36 can be best appreciated by considering the 2.13m/7ft-high tunnel that passed within the wings to allow inflight maintenance of the outer engines.**

## Convair B-36J Peacemaker

**First flight:** August 8, 1946 (YB-36)
**Power:** Six Pratt & Whitney 3600hp R-4360-53 radial piston engines and four General Electric 2452kg/5400lb thrust J47-19 turbojets
**Armament:** Sixteen 20mm/0.78in cannon in fuselage tail and nose turrets; maximum bomb load of 20,884kg/46,000lb
**Size:** Wingspan – 70.1m/230ft
　　　Length – 49.4m/162ft 1in
　　　Height – 14.22m/46ft 8in
　　　Wing area – 443.32m²/4772sq ft
**Weights:** Empty – 77,650kg/171,035lb
　　　Maximum take-off – 186,140kg/410,000lb
**Performance:** Maximum speed – 661kph/411mph
　　　Service ceiling – 12,169m/39,900ft
　　　Range – 10,945km/6800 miles
　　　Climb – 677m/2220ft per minute

# Convair B-58 Hustler

TOP: **The creation of the B-58 required much new ground to be broken. The result was a potent high-performance weapon system.**
ABOVE: **Bombs, reconnaissance equipment and extra fuel could be carried in the Hustler's centreline pod.**

The delta-winged B-58 was designed as a supersonic replacement for the USAF's B-47, and the prototype's first flight took place on November 11, 1956. The aircraft went supersonic for the first time on December 30 that year. A total of 116 aircraft were built, including 30 test and pre-production aircraft, and the aircraft reached squadron service in 1960, becoming the Strategic Air Command's and the world's first operational supersonic bomber.

The B-58 was first designed to meet an exacting requirement, and the design team had to make great advances to meet it. The aircraft had to fly at Mach 2 (the first bomber to do so) at high-altitude, carry and accurately drop nuclear weapons, and be as small as possible to have the smallest possible radar signature. The aircraft, all of its equipment and weaponry were for the first time seen as an entire weapons system in USAF procurement, and Convair was responsible for making it all work together. This new approach required the breaking of much new ground, and did lead to delays.

There were many "firsts" associated with the B-58 Hustler. It was the first aircraft to have heat-resistant, stainless-steel honeycomb sandwich skin panels in the wings and fuselage, and was the first bomber with a weapons pod to be jettisoned after bombing. The B-58 was the first supersonic aircraft with engine pods mounted outboard on the thin delta wing, which had a 60-degree sweep.

Crew consisted of a pilot, navigator and defensive systems operator seated in tandem. Each crew member also had a unique escape ejection capsule – these were retrofitted when it was realized that simple ejection seats would not protect crews ejecting at supersonic speeds. To improve the crew's chances of surviving ejection, a high-speed, high-altitude capsule ejection system was installed that would allow safe ejection at supersonic speeds up to altitudes of 21,350m/70,000ft.

When required, the individual crew member's capsule closed airtight clam-shell doors, activating independent pressurization and oxygen supply systems. The crew member could then eject the capsule or remain encapsulated in the event of cabin pressure or oxygen loss until the aircraft reached a lower altitude. The pilot's capsule contained a control stick and other equipment so that he could continue to fly the aircraft from inside the capsule. After ejection, the capsule was lowered by parachute, and shock absorbers were included to soften the landing. On water, the airtight capsule would float, and additional flotation bags could turn the capsule into a life raft.

The thin fuselage had no room for a bomb bay, so the aircraft was fitted with a unique large streamlined centreline weapons pod, which included a fuel tank as well as a nuclear bomb or reconnaissance equipment. It was the pod and access to it on the ground that necessitated the B-58's very tall undercarriage legs. Four bombs could be carried beneath the wing if the pod was removed, but with the associated loss of a fuel tank, this could only have been over shorter ranges.

Although the Hustler had a greater range than the B-47 it was intended to replace, it still needed forward bases to be able to hit the Soviet Union. The alternative was to refuel the B-58 inflight to give it a greater reach, and all bomber versions were built with this facility. The B-58 set many high-speed records, flying for up 20 hours on routes around the world thanks to inflight refuelling. These missions were not just for the record books but also had some sabre-rattling potential, showing the Soviet Union just how far the aircraft could and would fly if needed. However, the B-58's range problem was made worse by the tactical need to bring the bombers down to low level. Soviet anti-aircraft missile defences were improving, so even the high- and fast-flying B-58 could not avoid them. As a result, the B-58 crews switched tactics and trained, very effectively, to penetrate Soviet defences at low level beneath enemy radar, resulting in an increase in fuel consumption and associated range penalties.

TOP: **This aircraft is a YB-58A production prototype. The non-standard red and white paint scheme identifies the aircraft as a test aircraft.** ABOVE: **The Hustler had to have long undercarriage legs to give clearance to the weapons pod.**

Eighty-six Hustlers were operational in Strategic Air Command from 1960, but the aircraft was phased out after only ten years due to high operating costs, operational limitations and the limited opportunities for development of the design. An interesting B-58 offshoot was a plan (which stayed on the drawing board) to produce a supersonic passenger-carrying version with a wider fuselage and room for 52 seats.

ABOVE: **The TB-58A was an operational trainer with the middle cockpit adapted for use by an instructor. Seven aircraft were converted to this standard. Notice how high the aircraft sits with the pod removed.**

## Convair B-58 Hustler

**First flight:** November 11, 1956
**Power:** Four General Electric 7082kg/15,600lb afterburning thrust J79-5B turbojets
**Armament:** One 20mm/0.78in cannon in tail; payloads (including pod) of up to 8830kg/ 19,450lb of nuclear or conventional weapons
**Size:** Wingspan – 17.32m/56ft 10in
Length – 29.49m/96ft 9in
Height – 9.58m/31ft5in
Wing area – 143.35m²/1543sq ft
**Weights:** Empty – 25224kg/55,560lb
Maximum take-off – 74,002kg/163,000lb
**Performance:** Maximum speed – 2128kph/ 1322mph
Ceiling – 19,520m/64,000ft
Range – 8248km/5125 miles
Climb – 5310m/17,400ft per minute

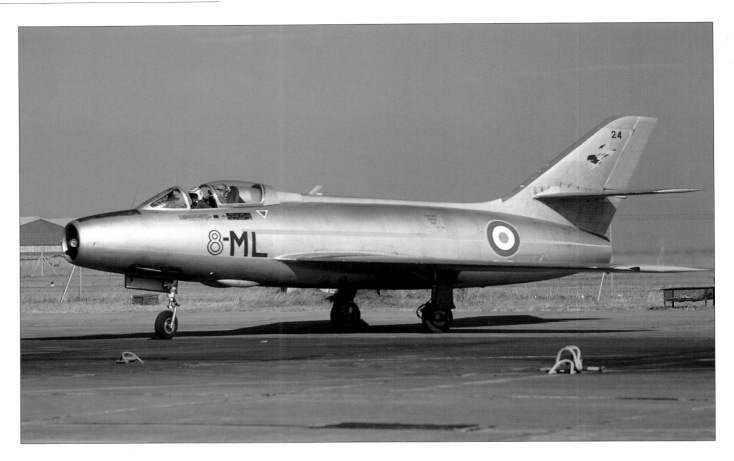

# Dassault Mystère/Super Mystère

Developed from the Dassault Ouragan, France's first jet fighter, the Mystère was essentially an Ouragan with swept wing and tail surfaces, and first flew in 1951. The production version, the Mystère II, was among the first swept-wing aircraft in production in western Europe, and entered Armée de l'Air service between 1954 and 1956 powered by the SNECMA Atar, the first French turbojet to be used in military aircraft. A Mystère IIA was the first French aircraft to break Mach 1

in controlled flight (in a dive), on October 28, 1952. The Armée de l'Air ordered 150 Mystère IICs, and the last was delivered in 1957, by which time the type was already being relegated to advanced training duties. Even as the Mystère was becoming operational, the better Mystère IV was already flying. Mystère IIs remained in use as advanced trainers until 1963.

The Mystère IV was a new aircraft, having few common parts with the Mark II – it had a new oval-section fuselage, thinner wings with greater sweep, and new tail surfaces. The first prototype was flown in September 1952, powered by a Hispano-built Rolls-Royce Tay 250 turbojet, as were the first 50 production examples – later examples were powered by the Hispano-Suiza Verdon. The production contract for 225 Mystère IVAs for the Armée de l'Air was paid for by the USA as part of the NATO Military Assistance Program. The first production Mystère IVA flew in late May 1954, and the type entered service with the Armée de l'Air the following year. The Mystère IVA remained a first-line fighter with the Armée de l'Air until the early 1960s, but continued to serve as an operational trainer until 1980.

ABOVE: **Marcel Dassault started to design jet fighters two years after being freed from a Nazi concentration camp. The Mystère was developed from his first design, the Ouragan, and ultimately led to the Mystère IVA pictured.**
LEFT: **The IVA was a very basic combat jet by today's standards, but it served the French Air Force well into the 1980s.**

ABOVE: **A Mystère IVA of the Armée de l'Air EC 8 (8th Fighter Wing). Note the open airbrakes.**
LEFT: **The ultimate Mystère – the Super Mystère first flew in 1955, and was exported to Honduras and Israel.** BELOW: **This Super Mystère was photographed at an annual NATO "Tiger Meet".**

Sixty Verdon-powered Mystère IVAs ordered by the French were sold on to Israel, and the first batch of 24 arrived in April 1956, just in time for the war with Egypt in October. In the hands of skilled Israeli pilots, they proved more than a match for Egyptian MiG-15s. The Indian Air Force also bought 110 all-new production Verdon-powered Mystère IVAs. First delivered in 1957, they equipped five squadrons and were used in the close-support role during the 1965 Indo-Pakistan war. Indian Mystère IVAs served until 1973.

The ultimate Mystère was the Super Mystère which, like the Mystère IV, was largely a new aircraft. It was bigger and heavier than previous Mystères and was the first European production aircraft capable of transonic flight. The first prototype flew in March 1955 and had wings with a 45-degree sweepback and an F-100-like oval air intake. The prototype exceeded Mach 1 in level flight the day after it first took to the air. A total of 180 Super Mystère B2s were built for the Armée de l'Air, the last delivered in 1959. They were switched to the attack role once the Mirage III was available, and remained in French service until late 1977.

In 1958, 36 Super Mystères bought by the French were sold on to the Israelis who used them to counter the Soviet-designed and built MiG-19s favoured by Arab nations. In the early 1970s, the Israelis upgraded surviving Super Mystères by retrofitting a non-afterburning Pratt & Whitney J52-P8A turbojet, and 12 of these uprated Super Mystères were sold to Honduras, who operated them until 1989. Their retirement brought the operational career of the Mystère series to an end.

## Dassault Mystère IVA

**First flight:** February 23, 1951 (Mystère prototype)
**Engine:** Hispano-Suiza 3500kg/7703lb thrust Verdon 350 turbojet.
**Armament:** Two 30mm/1.18in cannon; two 454kg/1000lb bombs or twelve rockets
**Size:** Wingspan 11.12m/36ft 6in
Length – 12.85m/42ft 2in
Height 4.60m/15ft 1in
Wing area – 32m²/344.46sq ft
**Weights:** Empty – 5886kg/12,955lb
Maximum take-off – 9500kg/20,909kg
**Performance:** Maximum speed – 1120kph/696mph
Ceiling – 15,000m/49,200ft
Climb – 2700m/8860ft per minute
Range – 912km/570 miles

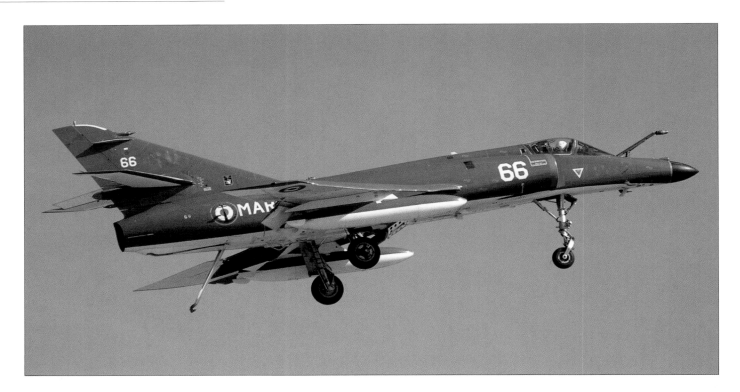

# Dassault Etendard and Super Etendard

Dassault's private venture Etendard (standard) was designed to meet the needs of both French national and NATO programmes for new light fighters reflecting air-combat experiences of the Korean War. Various versions did not get beyond the prototype stage, but then the Etendard IV drew the attention of the French Navy as a multi-role carrier-based fighter, leading to the development of the Etendard IV M specifically for the Navy – the first naval aircraft developed by Dassault.

The Etendard IV M made its maiden flight in May 1958, and between 1961 and 1965 the French Navy took delivery of 69 Etendard IV Ms that served on the French carriers *Foch* and *Clemenceau*, as well as 21 reconnaissance/tanker Etendard IV Ps. The Etendard IV M continued to serve in the French Navy until July 1991, by which time they had logged 180,000 flying hours and made 25,300 carrier landings.

The search for an Etendard replacement led Dassault to propose the Super Etendard, an updated, improved aircraft based on the Etendard IV M, but a 90 per cent new design.

Designed both for strike and interception duties, it featured the more powerful Atar 8K-50 engine and a strengthened structure to withstand higher-speed operations. The weapons system was improved through the installation of a modern navigation and combat management system centered on a Thomson multi-mode radar. The wing had a new leading edge and revised flaps which, together with the newer engine, eased take-off with greater weight compared to the Etendard.

The aircraft prototype made its maiden flight October 28, 1974, and the first of 71 production aircraft were delivered from mid-1978, again for service on the aircraft carriers *Foch*

TOP: **The Super Etendard was derived from the earlier Etendard, but was a 90 per cent new aircraft.** ABOVE: **The Etendard IVP had a fixed refuelling probe and could carry a "buddy pack" to become an inflight tanker.**

and *Clemenceau*. One hundred Super Etendards were planned for the Navy, but spiralling costs called for a reduction of the order. Armed with two 30mm/1.18in cannon, the Super Etendard could carry a variety of weaponry on its five hard points, including two Matra Magic AAMs, four pods of 18 68mm/2.68in rockets, a variety of bombs or two Exocet anti-ship missiles. A number were also modified to carry the Aerospatiale ASMP nuclear stand-off bomb.

The Argentine Navy's use of the Super Etendard/Exocet combination during the Falklands War of 1982 proved devastating against British ships – Argentina had ordered 14 Super Etendards from Dassault in 1979, but only five aircraft and reportedly five missiles had been delivered by the time France embargoed arms shipments to Argentina. These five strike fighters, despite having pilots unwilling to engage the agile British Harriers in air combat, nevertheless proved to be a very potent element of the Argentine inventory.

On May 4, 1982, two Super Etendards took off from a base in Argentina, preparing to attack the British task force. After three hours and an inflight refuelling, the aircraft located and launched an attack on the British ships. One of the Exocets found and severely damaged the frigate HMS *Sheffield*, which sank on May 10. On May 25, two Exocet-equipped Super Etendards again attacked the task force, this time sinking the *Atlantic Conveyor* with its cargo of nine helicopters.

A handful of Super Etendards were supplied to Iraq in October 1983 when the Iraqis were desperate to cripple Iran by attacking tankers in the Persian Gulf with Exocets. Around 50 ships were attacked in the Gulf in 1984, the majority of the actions apparently carried out by Iraqi Super Etendards.

Production of the Super Etendard ended in 1983, but from 1992 a programme of structural and avionics upgrading was undertaken to extend the service life of the "fleet" until 2008.

ABOVE RIGHT: **The Etendard flew on with the French Navy until 1991.**
RIGHT: **An excellent on-deck view showing French Etendards and Super Etendards at sea.** BELOW: **French Navy Super Etendards are expected to remain in service at least until 2008.**

### Dassault Super Etendard

**First flight:** October 28, 1974
**Power:** SNECMA 5000kg/11,005lb afterburning thrust Atar 8K-50 turbojet
**Armament:** Two 30mm/1.18in cannon; 2100kg/ 4622lb of weapons, including Matra Magic AAMs, AM39 Exocet ASMs, bombs and rockets
**Size:** Wingspan - 9.6m/31ft 6in
Length – 14.31m/46ft 11.5in
Height – 3.86m/12ft 8in
Wing area – 28.4m²/305.71sq ft
**Weights:** Empty – 6500kg/14,306lb
Maximum take-off – 12,000kg/26,412lb
**Performance:** Maximum speed – 1205kph/ 749mph
Ceiling – 13,700m/44,950ft
Range – 650km/404 miles
Climb – 6000m/19,685ft per minute

# Dassault Mirage III family

The delta-wing Mirage III was certainly one of the greatest combat aircraft ever, and was produced in greater numbers than any other European fighter. The success of this aircraft brought France to the forefront of the military aircraft industry. It started as a Dassault private venture, and first flew in November 1956, having benefited from the testing of the small Mirage I experimental delta aircraft. After some refinements to the wing design, it reached twice the speed of sound in level flight in October 1958. The aircraft's capability soon caught the attention of the French Air Force, who quickly ordered the high-performance aircraft. Foreign air forces were also very interested in the Mirage, and orders from Israel and South Africa followed in late 1960. By now the first production aircraft, the Mirage IIIC single-seat air defence fighter, was coming off the production line for the Armée de l'Air, and the first were delivered in July 1961.

The Mirage IIIE was a long-range fighter-bomber version powered by the SNECMA Atar 9C turbojet. While the IIIC was a dedicated interceptor, the IIIE was designed and equipped for both air defence and all-weather ground attack, and French versions were equipped to carry a nuclear bomb. It was widely exported and was also built under licence in Australia and Switzerland. Although France has retired its IIIs, many air forces still operate the type, having upgraded it in many ways – Swiss and Brazilian IIIs, for example, have acquired canard wings.

The IIIE spawned the Mirage 5 ground-attack fighter, essentially a simplified version designed as a daytime clear-weather ground-attack fighter in response to an Israeli Air Force request. The need for sophisticated radar was considered not to be so great in the Middle East, so when the Mirage 5 first flew in May 1967, it was minus the Cyrano radar. The delivery to Israel was stopped for political reasons by Charles de Gaulle, and the aircraft instead served as the Mirage 5F in the Armée de l'Air. Israel decided to go it alone and developed its Mirage III into the Kfir.

RIGHT: **A Swiss Mirage III demonstrates its dramatic rocket-assisted take-off technique.** BELOW: **An Armée de l'Air Mirage IIIE armed with an AS.37 anti-radar missile.**

## Dassault Mirage 50

**First flight:** May 1969
**Power:** One SNECMA 7210kg/15,869lb afterburning thrust Atar 9K-50 turbojet
**Armament:** Two 30mm/1.18in cannon; up to 4000kg/8804lb of rockets, bombs and guided weapons
**Size:** Wingspan – 8.22m/27ft
Length – 15.56m/51ft 1in
Height – 4.5m/14ft 9in
Wing area – 35m²/375sq ft
**Weights:** Empty – 7150kg/15,737lb
Maximum take-off – 14,700kg/32,354lb
**Performance:** Maximum speed – 2338kph/ 1452mph
Ceiling – 18,011m/59,094ft
Range – 2410km/1496 miles
Climb – 11,168m/36,642ft per minute

ABOVE LEFT: **The excellent Mirage III can carry up to 4000kg/8804lb of ordnance.** LEFT: **Although French Mirage IIIs were retired some time ago, the type remains in use in Switzerland and Brazil.** BELOW: **Swiss Mirage IIIs received a canard wing as part of an upgrade programme.** BOTTOM: **An early French Mirage III. This type was produced in greater numbers than any other fighter of the period.**

However, some 450 Mirage 5s were exported to other nations, and more advanced avionics were offered later. Belgium built their own Mirage 5 bombers and upgraded them in the 1990s to keep them flying until 2005.

The Mirage 50 multi-mission fighter was created by installing the more powerful Atar 9K-50 engine in a Mirage 5 airframe. It first flew in April 1979, and boasted head-up displays and a more advanced radar than the Mirage III. Chile and Venezuela both ordered Mirage 50s. Dassault offers the Mirage 50M upgrade for existing Mirage IIIs and 5s, but several operator nations have undertaken local upgrade programmes with improved avionics and the addition of canard foreplanes.

In the 1967 and 1973 Arab-Israeli wars, the Israeli Mirage IIIs outclassed Arab-flown MiGs and generated lots of export sales, but Mirage pilots admit that the type did not have a great sustained turn capability due to the aerodynamic idiosyncrasies of the delta wing. Indeed, three Mirages were shot down by comparatively pedestrian Iraqi Hunters during the Six Day War of 1967. Nevertheless, the Mirage III series gave many air forces their first combat aircraft capable of flying at twice the speed of sound, and many upgraded examples will be flying for some years.

# Dassault Mirage IV

The Mirage IV strategic nuclear bomber was developed in the late 1950s, following a 1954 decision that France wanted an independent nuclear deterrent force. The aircraft was a two-seat, twin-jet engine supersonic bomber with an effective range of up to 4500km/2795 miles but only with inflight refuelling. The delta wing of the Mirage IV clearly carried on that of the Mirage III, though on a much larger scale. The Mirage IV was developed as a weapon system, with Dassault being the prime contractor for the complete system – aircraft, navigation, attack management system, as well as the casing and release system for the nuclear bomb.

The Mirage IV 01 made its maiden flight powered by two 6000kg/13,206lb SNECMA Atar 09 turbojets on June 17, 1959, with Roland Glavany at the controls. In July the aircraft achieved speeds of Mach 1.9. Three pre-production aircraft were then built, the first taking to the air in October 1961, this time powered by 6400kg/14,086lb thrust Atar 9C engines. Each of the three aircraft was used for trials and development of the aircraft's navigation, inflight refuelling and bombing systems.

However, it was more than two and a half years before the first Mirage IV-A was delivered to the French Air Force in February 1964. At the time of its delivery, the Mirage IV was the only aircraft in the world that could fly at twice the speed

TOP: **The development of the Mirage IV enabled France to create its own nuclear deterrent force. From 1964 to 1996 these impressive bombers were France's airborne deterrent.** ABOVE: **With a wingspan less than 1m/3ft greater than that of a Spitfire, the Mirage IV was able to attain speeds in excess of Mach 2.**

of sound for sustained periods. Fifty Mirage IV-As were ordered in 1959 and a further 12 in 1964, and they were all delivered by 1966.

Assigned to French Strategic Air Command, CFAS (Commandement des Forces Aeriennes Stratégiques), nine and later six dispersed air bases housed these aircraft, which were France's airborne nuclear deterrent from 1964 until the Mirage IV was retired as a strategic bomber in 1996. The aircraft had dedicated KC-135FR tanker aircraft assigned to the Mirage IV units, although Mirage IVs could also be fitted with "buddy" inflight refuelling packs themselves. The aircraft were kept at readiness in hardened shelters from which they could start their take-off run. For short-field take-off, the aircraft were also fitted with 12 booster rockets, six beneath each wing, and special fast-drying chemicals were developed for hardening soft surfaces from which the heavy aircraft could then operate.

### Dassault Mirage IV-A

**First Flight:** June 17, 1959

**Power:** Two SNECMA 7000kg/15,407lb thrust Atar 9K turbojets

**Armament:** One 60-kiloton AN 22 nuclear bomb or one 30- or 150-kiloton 900kg/1980lb ASMP stand-off nuclear air-to-surface missile or up to 7200kg/15,847lb of conventional bombs or anti-radar missiles

**Size:** Wingspan – 11.85m/38ft 11in
Length – 23.5m/77ft 1in
Height – 5.65m/18ft 6in
Wing area – 78m²/839.6sq ft

**Weights:** Empty – 14,500kg/31,914lb
Maximum take-off – 31,600kg/69,551lb

**Performance:** Maximum speed – 2338kph/1451mph
Ceiling – 20,000m/65,620ft
Range – 2500km/1552 miles
Climb – 11,000m/36,090ft in 4 minutes, 15 seconds

ABOVE: **Some of the fleet were upgraded to IV-P standard, and could carry a stand-off weapon.** RIGHT: **Rocket-assisted take-off was required to get the aircraft airborne from shorter runways, and was important for dispersed operations.** BELOW: **A Mirage IV-A in full flight. The IV-As were kept in hardened shelters from which they could begin their take-off run.**

In common with other major air forces around the world, the French Air Force had to respond to the increased sophistication of air defences. As a result, they switched to flying their bombers at low level to avoid enemy radar and surface-to-air missiles. The Mirage IV's structure was modified to cope better with the stresses caused by high-speed, low-level flying and the 60 kiloton AN 22 nuclear weapon carried semi-recessed under the fuselage, and was modified for low-level use and to increase the chances of aircraft and crew survivability.

The aircraft were frequently upgraded during their time in service, and 12 were modified for the reconnaissance role by fitting cameras and SLAR (side-looking airborne radar).

Nineteen aircraft were modified to IVP standard in the late 1980s by the inclusion of inertial navigation and rear-warning radar. This version could also carry the Aerospatiale ASMP stand-off nuclear missile, which could be launched up to 250km/155 miles from the target. In June 1996, the Mirage IVPs were retired from the nuclear role and five aircraft were retained for strategic reconnaissance duties.

# de Havilland Venom

The Venom was proposed by de Havilland as a Vampire successor, and was initially designated Vampire FB.8. The aircraft had to be substantially altered to accommodate the new more powerful Ghost engine and so the aircraft was given its own identity – the Venom. The first production version, the FB.1, was delivered to the RAF in December 1951, followed by the improved ejection-seat-equipped FB.4 version. The Venom ultimately equipped 19 squadrons of the Royal Air Force, serving in Germany, India and the Far East. The Germany-based Venoms were a vital element of the West's Cold War defences at the time.

Licence-built versions were produced as FB.50s in Switzerland, where some remained in service until the early 1980s. British-built versions were also exported to Iraq and Venezuela.

Two-seat radar-equipped all-weather/nightfighter versions were also produced, and the Venom NF.2 entered RAF service in 1953. Emergency escape from this version was virtually impossible as there were no ejection seats for the two crew and the heavy hinged canopy had to be lifted manually. The NF.3 had an American radar and, perhaps more importantly for Venom nightfighter crews, a quick-release canopy.

The de Havilland Sea Venom FAW Mk 20 gave the Royal Navy an interim radar-equipped, all-weather fighter force between the piston-engined Sea Hornet and the appearance of the advanced Sea Vixen. Later improvements led to the FAW Mk 21 and 22. The Sea Venom was also operated by the Australian Navy, and in France SNCASE built a redesigned Sea Venom, including a single-seat version for the French Navy, who called it the Aquilon.

Royal Navy Sea Venoms, in concert with RAF Venom fighter-bombers, saw action during the Suez crisis in 1956.

TOP: **A Venom FB.4 wearing "Suez stripes".**
ABOVE RIGHT: **During the Suez operations, three squadrons of RAF Venom FB4s flew close air support missions.** ABOVE: **A Sea Venom FAW Mk 21.**

## de Havilland Venom FB.4

**First flight:** September 2, 1949 (Venom prototype)
**Power:** de Havilland 2406kg/5300lb thrust Ghost 105 turbojet
**Armament:** Four 20mm/0.78in cannon; provision for two Firestreak air-to-air missiles or 908kg/2000lb of bombs or eight 27kg/60lb rocket projectiles
**Size:** Wingspan – 12.7m/41ft 8in
Length – 10.06m/33ft
Height – 2.03m/6ft 8in
Wing area – 25.99m²/279.75sq ft
**Weights:** Empty – 3995kg/8800lb
Maximum take-off – 6950kg/15,310lb
**Performance:** Maximum speed – 961kph/597mph
Ceiling – 14,640m/48,000ft
Range – 1730km/1075 miles
Climb – 36.7m/7230ft per minute

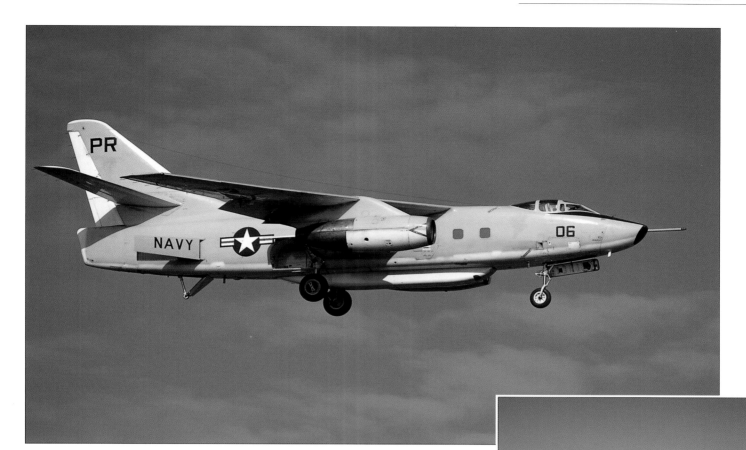

# Douglas A-3 Skywarrior

In the late 1940s, a whole new class of aircraft carrier was under development by the US Navy, the super-carrier Forrestal-class. These large carriers would be able to operate large aircraft and give the US Navy the opportunity to take its air power to a new level. The Navy called for a large new strategic bomber to operate from the supercarriers, and Douglas came up with the A3D, at 31,780kg/70,000lb the world's largest and heaviest carrier-borne aircraft when it was designed. It flew in October 1952, and became the Navy's first twin-jet nuclear bomber.

The nuclear bomb aspect was challenging because details of the weapon were top secret, and designers had to guess the appearance and weight of the nuclear bombs to be carried aboard. In its vast internal bomb bay it could carry up to 5448kg/12,000lb of weaponry. Also, the internal bomb bay had to be accessible from the cockpit so that the crew could arm the nuclear device during flight.

Due to its size, it was soon named "Whale" by its crews, and in 1962 the aircraft was redesignated A-3.

The first production version, the A-3A (A3D-1), with a radar-controlled tail turret and a crew of three, entered service with the Navy Heavy Attack Squadron One in 1956. After flying a few conventional bombing missions over North and South Vietnam, Skywarriors were used as carrier-based aerial-refuelling tankers and as reconnaissance aircraft covering the Ho Chi Minh trail. As advancing technology rendered its old role obsolete, the resilient aircraft continued to evolve. It was used for electronic countermeasures, photographic reconnaissance, crew training and as a VIP transport. A few US Navy Skywarriors even served in the 1991 Gulf War.

A revised USAF version was named Destroyer, and designated B-66. Built in bomber, photo-reconnaissance, electronic countermeasures and weather reconnaissance versions, the B-66 was active in the Vietnam War.

TOP: **The largest and heaviest carrier aircraft of its day, the A-3 Skywarrior.** ABOVE: **The "Whale" was a significant element of the US nuclear deterrent for a time.**

## Douglas A-3B Skywarrior

**First Flight:** October 28, 1952 (XA3D-1)

**Power:** Two Pratt & Whitney 4767kg/10,500lb thrust J57-P-10 turbojets

**Armament:** Two 20mm/0.78in cannon in remotely controlled rear turret; up to 5448kg/12,000lb of bombs

**Size:** Wingspan – 22.1m/72ft 6in
Length – 23.27m/76ft 4in
Height – 6.95m/22ft9.5in
Wing area – 75.43m²/812sq ft

**Weights:** Empty – 17,891kg/39,409lb
Maximum take-off – 37,228kg/82,000lb

**Performance:** Maximum speed – 982kph/610mph
Ceiling – 12,505m/41,000ft
Range – 1690km/1050 miles
Climb – 1100m/3600ft per minute

# Douglas Skyraider

The Skyraider can be rightly considered to be one of the greatest combat aircraft ever. Designed during World War II as a replacement for Douglas's own Dauntless dive-bomber, this rugged aeroplane fought in both Korea and Vietnam. The prototype XBT2D-1 first flew on March 19, 1945, and in February 1946 became the AD-1 Skyraider, the biggest single-seat aircraft in production. Designed around Wright's R-3350 engine, the Skyraider was created with the benefit of considerable combat experience. The designers' aim was to produce a very versatile aircraft which could absorb considerable damage and carry the widest range of available weaponry. Built like a big fighter, the Skyraider carried all of its weaponry beneath its folding wings.

Following carrier trials in early 1946, the Skyraider formally entered US Navy front-line service with VA-19A in December 1946. Production of consistently improved versions continued, and four years into manufacturing, 22 variants had appeared. Production continued for 12 years, and when it ceased in 1957, 3180 Skyraiders had been delivered to the US Navy.

Korea is often thought of as a jet war, but the Skyraider's 10-hour loiter capability and great weapon-carrying capacity considerably outclassed any jet then in service. The US Navy was hugely impressed by its performance.

Among the versions soon appearing were the AD-2 with increased fuel and a more powerful engine, and the AD-3 with a revised canopy, improved propeller and landing gear. The AD-4 had the more powerful 2700hp R-3350 engine and greatly increased load-carrying capacity, the AD-4W was a three-seat airborne early warning variant (used by the Royal

TOP: **A Royal Navy Skyraider AEW1. The type equipped two Fleet Air Arm units until 1960, and was used during the November 1956 Suez campaign.**
ABOVE: **Skyraiders were at home carrying out high-risk low-level missions. Here, an AD-1 drops napalm in Vietnam.**

Navy Fleet Air Arm), while the AD-5 was a four-seat, multi-role version. The Skyraider was strengthened to carry more and more equipment and ordnance, and the AD-5 could operate at all-up weights of 11,350kg/25,000lb. The AD-5 could also be adapted for casualty evacuation or for transporting 12 troops. The AD-6 was a much-improved single-seat attack version, while the AD-7 had a 3050hp engine and even more reinforcement to the wings and undercarriage.

**Douglas A-1H (AD-6) Skyraider**

**First Flight:** March 19, 1945 (XBT2D-1)
**Power:** One Wright 2700hp R-3350-26WA radial piston engine
**Armament:** Four wing-mounted 20mm/0.78in cannon; up to 3632kg/8000lb of ordnance carried under wings and on one fuselage hardpoint
**Size:** Wingspan – 15.25m/50ft 0.25in
    Length – 11.84m/38ft
    Height – 4.78m/15ft 8.25in
    Wing area – 37.19m²/400sq ft
**Weights:** Empty – 5433kg/11,968lb
    Maximum take-off – 11,350kg/25,000lb
**Performance:** Maximum speed – 518kph/322mph
    Ceiling – 8692m/28,500ft plus
    Range – 2116km/1315 miles
    Climb – 870m/2850ft per minute

ABOVE: **Fifty-four airframes were converted to EA-1F standard for electronic countermeasures duties.** LEFT: **The AD-4 version was built to carry a much greater war load, and the AD-4B was cleared to carry nuclear weapons.** BELOW: **Thought obsolete by doubters even before it entered service, the Skyraider confounded everyone with a production run in a myriad of variants and an outstanding combat record in two major conflicts.**

AD-4Ns saw considerable action with the French Armée de l'Air in Algeria, and these machines were retired in 1965. By now the USA was embroiled in Vietnam, and following trials the Skyraider was found to be the ideal close support aircraft needed for tackling difficult ground targets. Again, the hard-hitting aircraft's loiter capability made it an obvious choice for this type of warfare. The US Air Force, Navy and Marine Corps all operated Skyraiders in Vietnam, as did the US-trained South Vietnam Air Force. The aircraft also served as forward air control (FAC) platforms, helicopter escort and rescue support missions. Never considered a dogfighter, the Skyraider had four 20mm/0.78in cannon in the wings, and US Navy Skyraider pilots are known to have shot down at least two MiG-17 jets over Vietnam.

In 1962, new tri-service aircraft designations were introduced so all the designations of Skyraiders then in service were changed. The AD-5 was the A-1E, the AD-5N the A-1G while the AD-6 and AD-7 became the A-1H and A-1J respectively.

As well as Britain and France, Skyraiders were also supplied to Chad, who used them in combat up to the late 1970s. The aircraft that had entered service when piston-engined warplanes were considered by some to be obsolete was therefore still fighting more than a quarter of a century after it first entered service.

ABOVE: **The A-1E/AD-5 was a redesigned multi-role aircraft with a side-by-side cockpit.**

67

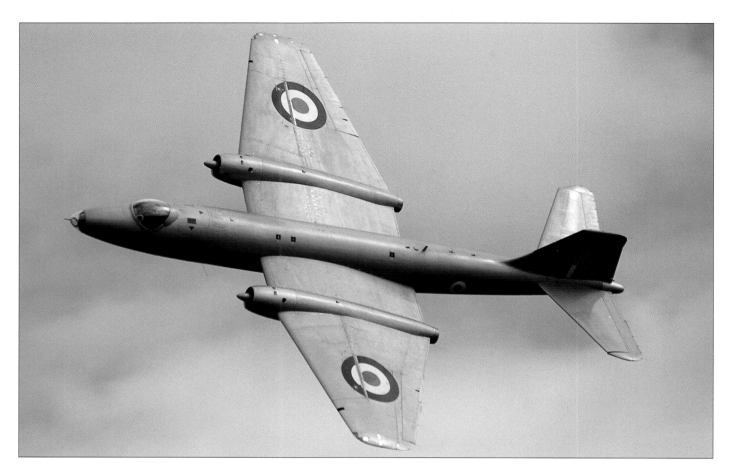

# English Electric/BAC/Martin B-57 Canberra

When it comes to long-service records in the Royal Air Force, there is one aircraft that leads the field – the English Electric Canberra. More than half a century after the type first entered RAF service in 1950, photo-reconnaissance versions continue to be a vital element of the RAF's intelligence-gathering capability.

The Canberra was Britain's first jet bomber and was designed in the Mosquito tradition, so that its high and fast flying capability was intended to keep the aircraft safe from defending fighter aircraft – no defensive armament was to

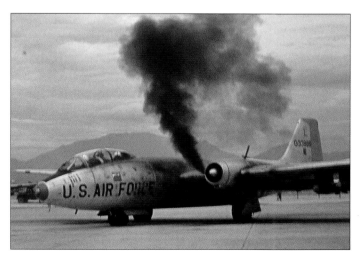

be carried. The Canberra was every bit as versatile as the Mosquito it succeeded, and served with distinction as a light bomber, advanced trainer, intruder and photo-reconnaissance platform.

The first Canberra prototype, VN799, took off from Warton on May 13, 1949, with famous test-pilot Roland Beamont at the controls. It exhibited excellent manoeuvrability at all altitudes and handled well at low speed. Refinements to the original design led to the B.2 version, which first flew in April 1950 and became the RAF's first jet bomber when it entered service at RAF Binbrook in May 1951 with No.101 Squadron. The RAF needed lots of Canberras, and production was beyond the capability of English Electric. Consequently, rival manufacturers Avro, Handley Page and Shorts all built Canberras to meet the demand. A more powerful version, the B.6, entered RAF service in 1954–5, and Canberras saw combat over Malaya and during the 1956 Suez Crisis.

An indication of the aircraft's greatness is the fact that early in its career, the Canberra was selected for licensed production in the USA for the US Air Force. The first of

TOP: **WK163 was a Canberra B.2 that was fitted with Scorpion rocket engines to attain a record-breaking altitude.** LEFT: **The USAF sought an aircraft with good manoeuvrability and flexibility, and found it in the Canberra. Licence-built as the Martin B-57 Canberra, around 400 were built in the USA.**

around 400 aircraft (bomber and reconnaissance versions) was rolled out of the Martin plant on July 20, 1953. These American Canberras saw extensive service in Vietnam.

Canberras were also built under licence in Australia for the RAAF. These versions, known as MK20s, were based on the British B.2 version but had increased internal fuel capacity and a crew of two. In September 1958 Canberras from No.2 Squadron RAAF became the first Australian jet bombers in combat when they carried out an attack against terrorists in Northern Malaya. Then in 1967, No.2 was sent to Vietnam as part of Australia's military commitment to the war. Operating as part of the USAF's 35th Tactical Fighter Wing, Squadron 2's Canberras flew 6 per cent of the Wing's sorties but inflicted 16 per cent of the damage. Overall, 11,963 sorties were flown in Vietnam, and 76,389 bombs dropped for two aircraft lost.

The Canberra's distinguished RAAF career ended on June 30, 1982, when No.2 Squadron flew its Canberras for the last time.

English Electric and its subcontractors built over 750 Canberras, and many were exported. In the early 2000s, Canberra remained in service with Argentina, India, Peru and even NASA (B-57s).

Photo-reconnaissance versions were developed early on, and it was the PR.9 version that remained in service with the RAF in 2004. In 2003, Canberras of No.39 Squadron conducted 56 reconnaissance sorties over Iraq in support of British and Coalition forces.

The PR.9's equipment had evolved over its time in service. A variety of daytime "wet" cameras can be carried for medium and higher-level vertical and oblique photography. An electro-optical long-range oblique photographic sensor (EO-LOROP) can also be carried, which records imagery in digital format on magnetic tape for interpretation on the ground. The PR.9 also carries navigation equipment that 1960s navigators could only have dreamt of, as well as defensive systems such as jammers and chaff and flare dispensers.

ABOVE: **USAF B-57s saw extensive use in the Vietnam War, mainly flying night intruder missions. The aircraft pictured here is a multi-role bomber/reconnaissance/trainer/tug B-57E.** RIGHT: **When the RAF Canberra's bombing days were over, some were converted for ECM training. The aircraft in this photograph is a T.17.** BELOW: **The Canberra is an all-time classic combat aircraft. This model is an E.15 used for high-altitude calibration of ground radar.**

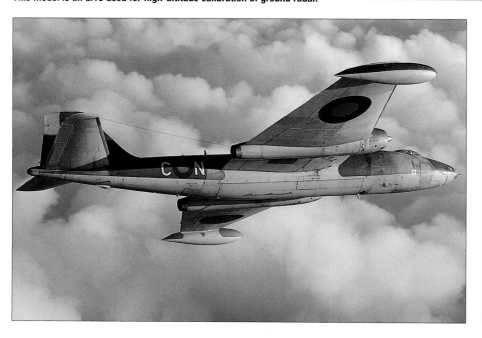

### English Electric/BAC Canberra B.6

**First Flight:** May 13, 1949 (prototype)
**Power:** Two Rolls-Royce 3405kg/7500lb afterburning thrust Avon 109 turbojets
**Armament:** 2724kg/6000lb of bombs carried internally, plus two 454kg/1000lb bombs or gun pods under wings
**Size:** Wingspan 19.51m/64ft
Length – 19.96m/65ft 6in
Height – 4.75m/15ft 7in
Wing area – 89.19m²/960sq ft
**Weights:** Empty – 10,108kg/22,265lb
Maximum take-off – 24,062kg/53,000lb
**Performance:** Maximum speed – 973kph/605mph
Ceiling – 14,634m/48,000ft plus
Combat radius – 1779km/1105 miles
Climb – 1220m/4000ft per minute

# Fairchild Republic A-10 Thunderbolt II

In the early 1970s, when the USAF was considering an aircraft capable of halting a Soviet armoured thrust in Central Europe, they looked back at their experiences in Korea and Vietnam where aircraft modified for use in the close air support role had exhibited many shortcomings. Instead, they needed a purpose-designed aircraft that could carry a heavy weapons load, have good endurance and be able to withstand damage from ground fire.

The answer was the remarkable A-10, designed from the outset to tackle Warsaw Pact armour in Europe. Combining accurate firepower and survivability, the A-10 was designed to fly low and relatively slowly across the battlefield to take out enemy armour and artillery in the very hostile, low-level battlefield environment. The aircraft has high-lift wings fitted with large control surfaces, making the aircraft very manoeuvrable, while its short take-off and landing capability permitted operations in and out of rough field locations near front lines.

All the aircraft's controls are duplicated and designed to work even if hydraulic pressure is lost due to enemy fire. The aircraft's fuel tanks are filled with fire-retardant foam, and the A-10's pilot sits in a "bathtub" of titanium armour for protection against shrapnel and small arms fire.

The aircraft can survive direct hits from armour-piercing and high explosive projectiles up to 23mm/0.9in calibre. Self-sealing fuel cells are protected by internal and external foam. Remarkably, many of the aircraft's parts are interchangeable left and right, including the engines, main landing gear and fins.

TOP: **The arrival of the A-10 over a battlefield is bad news for an enemy. The aircraft was created to destroy armour and artillery, and does so most effectively.** ABOVE: **This view shows how the aircraft's engines can be masked by the wing from below, thus preventing a lock from an infrared weapon.**

The primary weapon of the A-10 is the nose-mounted GAU-8/A 30mm/1.18in seven-barrel cannon which, together with its ammunition, takes up much of the aircraft's internal space. This is the most powerful gun ever fitted to an aircraft, firing 35 rounds of controversial depleted uranium armour-piercing ammunition per second. One hit from this extremely potent weapon can destroy a tank a mile away from the aircraft. The aircraft can also carry a range of bombs, rockets and missiles, including the Maverick anti-armour missile.

LEFT: **Designed to halt Soviet armour, the A-10 entered front-line service in 1976. Note the 30mm/1.18in cannon protruding from the nose.**
BELOW: **Feeding the beast – belts of 30mm/1.18in ammunition are loaded for the A-10's devastating 30mm/1.18in cannon. 1350 rounds are carried.**

ABOVE: **This A-10 is carrying Sidewinder air-to-air missiles for self defence. Eleven hardpoints can carry an array of ground-attack weaponry.**
RIGHT: **The A-10 is likely to remain in service until at least 2010.**

Turbofan engines were chosen to power the aircraft because they give off less heat than conventional jet engines, thus making them less vulnerable to heat-seeking weapons. The engines were also positioned high on the upper rear fuselage, protecting them from ground fire. Using night-vision goggles, A-10 pilots can conduct their missions as efficiently during darkness as in daylight.

The A-10 entered US Air Force service in 1976 and remained in the Cold War front line until the late 1980s. Although trained for war in Europe, USAF A-10 pilots first saw action in the Gulf War of 1991 when 144 A-10s were deployed to Saudi Arabia. During the A-10's 8100 Gulf War missions, around 24,000 missiles, rockets and bombs were fired or dropped and one million rounds were fired by A-10 cannon. A-10s launched 90 per cent of the total number of the AGM-65 Maverick missiles used.

USAF A-10s were credited with the destruction of over 1000 Iraqi tanks, 1200 artillery pieces and 2000 vehicles, as well as two helicopters in air-to-air combat with air-to-air missiles. Only six aircraft were lost in the war, all to ground-launched enemy missiles.

A-10s were also in the vanguard of the 2003 invasion of Iraq, and are expected to remain in the USAF inventory until 2010.

## Fairchild Republic A-10 Thunderbolt II

**First Flight:** May 10, 1972
**Power:** Two General Electric 4115kg/9065lb thrust TF34-GE-100 turbofans
**Armament:** One GAU-8/A 30mm/1.18in cannon; up to 7264kg/16,000lb of weapons, including free-fall or guided bombs, Maverick missiles or Sidewinder anti-aircraft missiles on underwing and underfuselage points
**Size:** Wingspan – 17.53m/57ft 6in
Length – 16.26m/53ft 4in
Height – 4.42m/14ft 8in
Wing area – 24.18m²/260.28sq ft
**Weights:** Empty – 9780kg/21,541lb
Maximum take-off – 22,700kg/50,000lb
**Performance:** Maximum speed – 706kph/439mph
Ceiling – 9302m/30,500ft plus
Range – 926km/576 miles
Climb – Not available

# Fairey Gannet

During the course of World War II, the Royal Navy had learned the value of carrier-based anti-submarine aircraft. For the post-war years the Navy needed a modern aircraft to tackle the submarine threat posed by any potential enemy. In 1945 the Fleet Air Arm issued a requirement, GR.17/45, for a carrier-based ASW (anti-submarine warfare) aircraft which could both hunt and kill submarines.

Of two cosmetically similar designs built to prototype standard, it was the Fairey design that ultimately won the contract, having flown for the first time on September 19, 1949. The aircraft had a deep barrel-like fuselage to accommodate both sensors and weapons for hunting and killing enemy craft. Power came from an Armstrong-Siddeley Double Mamba engine which was actually two turboprop engines driving a shared gearbox. This in turn drove a contra-rotating propeller system. The Double Mamba was chosen because one of the engines could be shut down for more economical cruising flight. Conventional twin-engined aircraft exhibit problematic handling if one engine fails, resulting in what is known as asymmetric flight. In this situation, the working engine forces its side of the aeroplane ahead of the other side, resulting in crabbing flightpath, as well as major concerns on landing. If one Double Mamba failed, this would not be an issue for the pilot of a Gannet.

The Fairey 17 began carrier-deck trials in early 1950, and on June 19 that year the aircraft made the first landing of a turboprop aircraft on a carrier, HMS *Illustrious*. The Admiralty then requested that search radar be included, as well as a

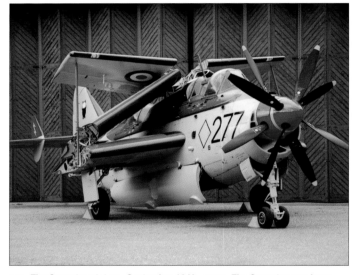

TOP: **The Gannet prototype, September 1949.** ABOVE: **The Gannet was a large aircraft and the wings had to fold twice to fit it into underdeck hangars.**

third seat for the operator, resulting in a third modified prototype which flew in May 1951. When Fairey's aircraft won the competition to go into production, the name "Gannet" was given to the aircraft. The Gannet, brimming with equipment and weapons, was a technically complicated aircraft, an example being the wings that folded not once but twice for under-deck stowage. Because of development delays, the Gannet AS.1 did not enter FAA service until 1955, some ten years after the requirement was first issued.

The fuselage had a big weapons bay to accommodate two torpedoes or other munitions, up to a total of 908kg/2,000lb. A retractable radome under the rear fuselage housed the search radar. When the extendable "dustbin" radome was added, it led to lateral instability in flight, which was remedied by the addition of two auxiliary finlets to the horizontal tailplane. Simply raising the height of the vertical tailplane would have had the same effect, but would have exceeded below-deck hangar height limits. The Gannet's crew of three sat in tandem, with pilot, observer/navigator and radio/radar operator each in their own cockpits, the radio/radar operator's seat facing the tail of the aircraft.

A number of Gannets were operated by foreign air arms. Deliveries to the Royal Australian Navy for carrier operations began in 1955 (phased out in 1967), while the former West German naval air arm operated Gannets from shore bases, phasing them out in 1965. Indonesia obtained refurbished Royal Navy examples.

A total of 181 Gannet AS.1s were built, together with 38 Gannet T.2 conversion trainers for training pilots on the idiosyncrasies of the aircraft and its unique powerplant. In 1956, the improved 3035hp Double Mamba 101 was introduced into Gannets on the production line. Aircraft thus powered were designated AS.4 and T.5 for the trainer version. The Gannet AS.6 was the AS.4 with a new 1961 radar and electronics fit.

Fairey were also contracted to produce an airborne early warning (AEW) Gannet to replace the Douglas Skyraider in Fleet Air Arm service. Designated AEW.3, these were new-build dedicated early-warning aircraft with a huge radar installation mounted on the underside of the fuselage beneath the cockpit. This version, which served until 1977, carried a pilot and two radar plotters who were housed in a rear cabin.

ABOVE: **Points to note on this Gannet AS.4 are the large port exhaust from the Double Mamba, the arrestor hook and the two red finlets.** BELOW: **Note the large radome beneath the Gannet AEW.3.** BOTTOM: **The AEW Gannets were retired from RN service in 1977.**

### Fairey Gannet AS.1

**First flight:** September 19, 1949 (prototype)

**Power:** One Armstrong Siddeley 2950eshp Double Mamba 100 turboprop

**Armament:** Up to 908kg/2000lb of torpedoes and depth charges

**Size:** Wingspan – 16.56m/54ft 4in
Length – 13.11m/43ft
Height – 4.18m/13ft 8.5in
Wing area – 44.85m²/482.8sq ft

**Weights:** Empty – 6841kg/15,069lb
Maximum take-off – 9806kg/21,600lb

**Performance:** Maximum speed – 499kph/310mph
Ceiling – 7625m/25,000ft
Range – 1518km/943 miles
Climb – 670m/2200ft per minute

# General Dynamics F-111

The F-111 was originally intended to be a fighter to equip both the US Air Force and Navy. Following a difficult development period during which the Navy dropped out of the programme, the remarkable variable-geometry aircraft, with its confusing fighter designation, became a highly effective all-weather interdictor.

The F-111 was the first production aircraft in the world with "swing wings", which gave the aircraft the flexibility to land and take off with straight wings and for low-speed flight, but to fly at high supersonic speeds with the wings swept.

TOP: **An Upper Heyford-based F-111E launches an attack on a British bombing range.** ABOVE: **The F-111 terrain-following radar enables the aircraft to fly very fast and very low to deliver its weapons.**

The F-111A entered USAF service in October 1967. Once early in-service problems were ironed out, the F-111 became a formidable long-range bomber which could deliver conventional or nuclear weapons from low altitude. The F-111 weapons system also featured a groundbreaking automatic terrain-following radar that guided the aircraft at a pre-set height following the ground contours. The aircraft could fly itself over all types of terrain by day or night, whatever the weather.

The wings and much of the fuselage rear of the crew compartment contained fuel tanks. Using internal fuel only, the aircraft had a range of more than 4000km/2500 miles. External fuel tanks could be carried on the wing pylons for additional range, and could be jettisoned if necessary.

The F-111 could deliver conventional or nuclear weapons and could carry up to two bombs or additional fuel in the internal weapons bay. External ordnance included combinations of bombs, missiles and fuel tanks. The loads nearest the fuselage on each side pivoted as the wings swept back, keeping ordnance parallel to the fuselage. Outer pylons did not move, but could be jettisoned for high-speed flight.

The F-111E model had modified air intakes to improve the engine's performance at speeds above Mach 2.2. Most USAF F-111Es served with the 20th Fighter Wing based at RAF Upper Heyford, England, in support of NATO. On January 17, 1991, F-111Es deployed to Incirlik Air Base, Turkey, carried out some of the first bombing raids of Operation Desert Storm. More than 100 F-111 aircraft of different versions joined the first strikes against Iraqi targets, both as bombers and radar jammers. As the war progressed, the F-111s were employed in precision attacks with laser-guided weapons on hardened aircraft shelters and bunkers. Later in the war, the F-111s were used against enemy tanks at night.

The F-111F had improved turbofan engines, giving 35 per cent more thrust than those of the F-111A and E. The last F-model was delivered to the Air Force in November 1976. The F-model equipped RAF Lakenheath's 48th Fighter Wing, and had been proven in combat over Libya in 1986.

Development of the EF-111A Raven began in January 1975 when the Air Force made a contract with Grumman Aerospace to modify two F-111As to serve as electronic warfare platforms.

One of the F-111's design innovations was its unique crew escape module, a requirement stipulated by the US Navy but retained in the ultimate Air Force model. The pilot and weapons system officer sit side by side in the

air-conditioned, pressurized module and therefore have no requirement for ejection seats or pressure suits. If the crew pulled the "eject" handles on the centre console, a rocket motor blasts the "pod" clear of the aircraft and it descends by parachute. The module could be fired even at ground level or under water. Flotation bags were fitted to the watertight and airtight module for a water landing.

F-111Cs were an export version supplied to the Royal Australian Air Force, the F-111's only export client. When production ceased in 1976, a total of 562 F-111s had been built.

TOP RIGHT: **The F-111 was the first production aircraft with a variable sweep wing.** ABOVE: **The RAAF was the only non-US operator of the F-111.**
RIGHT: **An F-111 with wings unswept for relatively low-speed flight.**
BELOW: **The crew escape module was one of the F-111's many innovations.**

## General Dynamics F-111F

**First flight:** December 21, 1964 (F-111A)
**Power:** Two Pratt & Whitney 11,395kg/25,100lb afterburning thrust TF30-P-100 turbofans
**Armament:** One 20mm/0.78in cannon; one 340kg/750lb nuclear or conventional bomb or two 340kg/750lb bombs in internal bomb bay, plus up to 11,350kg/25,000lb of bombs, rockets, missiles or fuel tanks on four under-wing pylons
**Size:** Wingspan – 19.2m/63ft, spread 9.74m/32ft, swept
Length – 22.4m/73ft 6in
Height – 5.22m/17ft 1in
Wing area – 48.77m²/525sq ft
**Weights:** Empty – 21,417kg/47,175lb
Maximum take-off – 45,400kg/100,000lb
**Performance:** Maximum speed – 2655kph/1650mph
Service ceiling – 17,995m/59,000ft plus
Range – 4707km/2925 miles
Climb – 6710m/22,000ft per minute

# Grumman A-6 Intruder/EA-6 Prowler

The Grumman A-6 Intruder, a two-seat, all-weather, subsonic, carrier-based attack aircraft, was designed for a 1957 US Navy competition for a new long-range, low-level tactical strike aircraft. While the performance of the subsonic A-6 was not spectacular, it was superbly suited to the particular attack role for which it was carefully tailored. The A-6 prototype made its first test-flight in April 1960, and was followed by 482 production A-6As delivered to the US Navy from early 1963. From night flights over the jungles of Vietnam to Desert Storm missions above heavily-fortified targets in Iraq, the Grumman A-6 Intruder developed a work-horse reputation, and was the subject of many tales of daring aviation during its 34-year career as the US Navy's principal medium-attack aircraft. The aircraft's ruggedness and all-weather mission capability made it a formidable asset to US Navy and Marine Corps air wings throughout its service. The strengths of the Intruder included its capability to fly in any weather and its heavy weapons payload – two traits highlighted on the big screen in the action film "Flight of the Intruder". A little-known fact is that the Intruder delivered more ordnance during the Vietnam War than the B-52.

A tough and versatile aircraft, the A-6 was called upon to fly the most difficult missions, with flying low and alone in any weather its speciality. The all-weather attack jet saw action in every conflict the USA has been involved in since Vietnam. With the ability to carry more ordnance, launch a wider variety of state-of-the-art smart weapons, conduct day or night strikes over greater distances on internal fuel than any carrier-borne aircraft before or since, and provide mid-air refuelling

TOP AND ABOVE: **The Intruder served the US Navy and Marine Corps through Vietnam, the Libya raids and the Gulf War – it is one of the greatest combat aircraft.**

support to other carrier jets, the Intruder is considered by some to be the most versatile military aircraft of modern times.

In 1986 the A-6E, an advanced upgraded development of the A-6A, proved that it was the best all-weather precision bomber in the world in the joint strike on Libyan terrorist-related targets. With US Air Force F-111s, A-6E Intruders penetrated sophisticated Libyan air defence systems, which had been alerted by the high level of diplomatic tension and by rumours of impending attacks. Evading over 100 guided missiles, the strike force flew at low level in complete darkness, and accurately delivered laser-guided and other ordnance on target.

No guns of any kind were carried aboard the A-6, and the aircraft had no internal bomb bay. However, a wide variety of stores could be mounted externally, including both conventional and nuclear bombs, fuel tanks and an assortment of rockets and missiles. As with all versatile attack aircraft, many combinations of payload and mission radius were available to the A-6E. For example, a weapons load of 945kg/2080lb, consisting of a Mark 43 nuclear bomb, could be delivered at a mission radius of 1432km/890 miles. For that mission, four 1362 litre/300 gallon external tanks would have been carried. Alternatively, a bomb load of 4648kg/10,296lb could be delivered at a mission radius of 724km/450 miles with two 1362 litre/300 gallon external tanks.

The EA-6B Prowlers were developed from the EA-6A, which was an Intruder airframe intended primarily to be an electronic countermeasures and intelligence-gathering platform. These aircraft were initially designed to fly in support of the Intruders on Vietnam missions. However, the EA-6B is a significant aircraft in its own right and provides an umbrella of protection for strike aircraft (by suppressing enemy air defences), ground troops and ships by jamming enemy radar, electronic data links and communications. At the same time, the Prowler is gathering tactical electronic intelligence within the combat area.

Intruders left US Navy service in the late 1990s but Prowlers will fly on for the foreseeable future.

ABOVE RIGHT: **The A-6 was responsible for dropping more bombs during the Vietnam War than the mighty B-52.**
RIGHT: **Note the fixed refuelling probe on the nose of this A-6.**
BELOW: **The Grumman Prowler was based on the Intruder, and has evolved into an aircraft which, in its own way, can disable enemy electronic defences.**

## Grumman A-6E Intruder

**First Flight:** April 19, 1960 (YA-6A)
**Power:** Two Pratt & Whitney 4222kg/9300lb thrust J52-P-8B turbojets
**Armament:** Up to 8172kg/18,000lb of nuclear or conventional ordnance or missiles
**Size:** Wingspan – 16.15m/53ft
Length – 16.69m/54ft 9in
Height – 4.93m/16ft 2in
Wing area – 49.13m²/528.9sq ft
**Weights:** Empty – 12104kg/26,660lb
Maximum catapult take-off – 26,604kg/58,600lb
**Performance:** Maximum speed – 1035kph/644mph
Ceiling – 12,932m/42,400ft
Range – 1627km/1011 miles
Climb – 2621m/8600ft per minute

# Handley Page Victor

It is hard to believe that while some at Handley Page were working on the Halifax during World War II, others were thinking about a tailless flying-wing jet-powered bomber. Shortly after the end of the war, the futuristic concept aroused the interest of the Air Ministry and the design evolved into an aircraft with a fuselage and a tail but with an innovative crescent-shaped wing. It took five years to get the design from the drawing board into the air – the prototype HP80 Victor WB771 took flight at Boscombe Down on Christmas Eve 1952.

As testing continued, more orders came from the RAF for the high-performance bomber, and in early 1956 the first Victor B.1 rolled off the production line. Capable of speeds in excess of the speed of sound in a shallow dive, the first Victors were delivered to the RAF in November 1957, and Bomber Command declared them operational in April 1958 with No.10 Squadron. The second production batch had a larger tailcone to accommodate tail warning radar, and refined engines, and these aircraft were designated B.1A. The Victor was now a nuclear bomber and part of Britain's V-force with the Vulcans and Valiants. However, with a bomb load of up to 15,890kg/ 35,000lb, the Victor could carry a much greater bomb load than the other V-bombers.

The improved Mk 2 variant with Rolls-Royce Conway engines (and thus redesigned wing roots and intakes), larger wing, modified tailcone and new electrical system among

TOP: **Painted in overall anti-flash white, the Victor, with the other V-bombers, was the UK's nuclear deterrent in the late 1950s.**

ABOVE: **The Victor's unusual crescent wing was groundbreaking. The Victor pictured here is a B(SR).2.**

other modifications, was finally put into production, and the first Victor B.2 flew in February 1959. As Soviet anti-aircraft defences improved, so the V-force had to modify its tactics to remain a credible deterrent. The B.2s became low-level, high-speed bombers, and also began to carry the Blue Steel stand-off nuclear missile.

The last B.2 was completed in April 1963, the year that RAF Victors were deployed to Singapore in a show of force to Indonesia, who threatened the British protectorate of Malaysia. As the B.2s replaced the earlier Marks in service, the B.1s and B.1As were converted into air-refuelling tankers (BK.1 and BK.1A).

LEFT: **Tanker trio – three Victors pictured a month before the type was retired in 1993.** BELOW LEFT: **Refuelling an RAF Jaguar en route to the Gulf, 1991.** BELOW: **This Victor K.2 is without its underwing refuelling pods. Note the large fuel tank hanging under the wing, and the inflight refuelling probe.**

### Handley Page Victor B. Mk 2

**First flight:** December 24, 1952

**Power:** Four Rolls-Royce 9352kg/20,600lb thrust Conway 201 turbofans

**Armament:** One Blue Steel stand-off missile or up to 15,890kg/35,000lb of conventional bombs

**Size:** Wingspan – 36.57m/120ft
Length – 35.03m/114ft 11in
Height – 8.57m/28ft 1.5in
Wing area – 241.3m²/2597sq ft

**Weights:** Empty – 51,864kg/114,240lb
Maximum take-off – 101,242kg/223,000lb

**Performance:** Maximum speed – 1038kph/645mph
Ceiling – 18,300m/60,000ft
Range – 7400km/4600 miles

The first converted Victor tanker flew on April 28, 1965. Special reconnaissance versions of the aircraft were also produced – nine B.2s were completed as B(SR).2s, and were excellent reconnaissance aircraft with bomb bays filled with cameras and massive flash units. The standard Victor remained in service as a nuclear bomber until 1975.

Further conversions of "surplus" Victor bombers resulted in the K.2 tanker, which entered service in May 1974. A total of 24 conversions were carried out, and the K.2s were expected to fly until around 1988.

It was as a tanker that the Handley Page bomber finally went to war. The very long-range 1982 Black Buck Vulcan bombing missions against Argentine forces on the Falklands were only possible due to 11 Victor tankers refuelling the bomber and themselves on the outward leg from Ascension. In a less well-known aspect of the Falklands campaign, Victor XH675 carried out a 11,263km/7000-mile, 14-hour and 45-minute reconnaissance mission, radar-mapping the South Atlantic.

The dwindling Victor tanker fleet was forced into the spotlight in early 1991 when coalition forces set about ousting Iraqi invaders from Kuwait. Eight tankers refuelled RAF and US combat aircraft on 299 sorties. The Victor was finally retired from RAF service on October 15, 1993. Eighty-six Victors had been produced in all.

# Hawker Siddeley/British Aerospace Nimrod

TOP: **The Nimrod is the only jet-powered, long-range maritime patrol and ASW aircraft.** ABOVE: **Somewhere in that shape lies the trailblazing de Havilland Comet jet airliner.**

Design work on the Nimrod began in June 1964 with the aim of replacing the RAF's ageing Shackleton maritime reconnaissance aircraft.

Based on the airframe of the world's first jet airliner, the de Havilland Comet, the production Nimrod was a new-build aircraft with a shorter, modified, pressurized fuselage. The addition of a weapons and operational equipment bay 15.8m/ 52ft in length under the main fuselage gave the aircraft its unique double-decker cross-section and enabled it to claim the biggest bomb bay of any NATO aircraft.

In 1965, the British Government gave the Nimrod project the go-ahead and two prototypes, conversions from civil Comets, first flew in 1967. The first production Nimrod MRI, XV226, had its maiden flight in June 1968 and the Nimrod entered Royal Air Force service in 1969.

The Nimrod was a revolutionary concept for a maritime patrol aircraft, a class typically powered by turboprops. The Nimrod combined the advantages of high altitude and comparatively high-speed capability from its jet powerplants coupled with low wing-loading and good low-level manoeuvrability.

The Nimrod has an enviable reputation for its anti-submarine warfare capabilities, surface surveillance and anti-shipping roles. In the anti-submarine warfare (ASW) role, prop-engined aircraft produce vibrations that are easily detectable by submarines, whereas the Nimrod's jet noise is virtually undetectable.

This very versatile aircraft can carry a variety of stores, including the Stingray torpedo, Harpoon anti-ship missile and Sidewinder infrared missile for self-defence or targets of opportunity. The aircraft can also carry its own chaff/flares suite for decoying incoming missiles.

### Hawker Siddeley/British Aerospace Nimrod MR2

**First Flight:** May 23, 1967

**Power:** Four Rolls-Royce 5511kg/12,140lb thrust Spey 250 turbofans

**Armament:** 6129kg/13,500lb of mixed maritime weaponry carried in bomb bay, including Harpoon anti-ship missiles, rocket/gun pods or pairs of Sidewinder AAMs carried under wing

**Size:** Wingspan – 35m/114ft 10in
Length – 38.63m/126ft 9in
Height – 9.05m/29ft 8.5in
Wing area – 197m²/2121sq ft

**Weights:** Empty – 39,362kg/86,700lb
Maximum take-off – 80,585kg/177,500lb

**Performance:** Maximum speed – 926kph/ 575mph
Ceiling – 12,810m/42,000ft
Range – 8045km/5000 miles plus
Climb – Not available

ABOVE: **The Nimrod's jet flight is difficult to detect from under water.**
RIGHT: **Note the inflight refuelling probe atop the nose and the magnetic anomaly detector boom projecting from the tail. The latter is just one means of detecting submerged submarines.**

In the early 1980s, the type was upgraded to MR2 standard, principally by updating and improving the aircraft's surveillance equipment. For the aircraft's role in Operation Corporate during the 1982 Falklands War, an inflight refuelling probe became standard. Royal Air Force Nimrods have seen service all over the world and played a pivotal role in the Falklands and Gulf conflicts.

The Nimrod currently carries out three main roles: anti-surface unit warfare (ASUW), anti-submarine warfare (ASW) and search-and-rescue (SAR). It has an unrefuelled endurance of around 10 hours.

After a quarter of a century in service, the Nimrod MR2's airframe and systems are to undergo a dramatic upgrade to MR4 standard, which will extend the type's operational life by a further 25 years. An 80 per cent new aircraft, the MR4 will be 30 per cent heavier than the MR2, carry 30 per cent more fuel and have twice the patrol endurance. The 18-strong fleet of MR4s is expected to be in service by 2009.

One less well-known aspect of the Nimrod story is the Nimrod R1. Three Nimrods were adapted to R1 standard in the early 1970s following the retirement of Comet 2Rs, and have been constantly upgraded ever since. The maritime reconnaissance equipment was removed and replaced with highly sophisticated and sensitive systems for reconnaissance and the gathering of electronic intelligence (ELINT). The ability of the Nimrod to loiter for long periods, following a high-speed dash to the required area of operation, makes the aircraft ideally suited to this task. RAF R1s have been quietly and secretly gathering information in trouble spots and on potential enemies of the UK since 1974.

ABOVE: **The Nimrod MR2 has a crew of 13 – three on the flight deck and the rest manning the banks of equipment carried on board.**

# Ilyushin Il-28

The Il-28 was the Soviet Air Force's first jet bomber to enter service. The aircraft, codenamed "Beagle" by NATO, has been described as Soviet's Canberra owing to its longevity and adaptability.

The Il-28 first flew on August 8, 1948, and the aircraft was in front-line service within two years. Twenty-five pre-production models took part in the 1950 Moscow May Day fly-past, an annual spectacle which was awaited with some trepidation on the part of western analysts during the Cold War. Production of this fine aircraft went on until around 1960, and some 10,000 were finally built by the Soviet Union and under licence in China until 1969. Design work on this medium bomber began around the end of World War II, and the aircraft's shape seemed to owe more to the past than the future. Straight-winged, the Il-28 did, however, have a highly swept-back tail fin and tailplanes for better control in high-speed dives.

Power for the prototype was provided by two RD-10 turbojets developed from wartime German Junkers Jumo engines, but production versions were powered by Klimov VK-1s, a Soviet version of the reliable British Nene engine supplied pre-Cold War.

The engines were mounted in pods beneath the wings in the same way that the Jumos had been mounted on the wartime Arado Blitz bomber. While the pilot had a rounded fighter-looking bubble canopy, the navigator/bombardier's bombsight was housed in a World War II-style greenhouse nose. At the base of the tail fin was a defensive powered gun turret which looked very similar to that of a B-17 or B-29, and housed two 23mm/0.9in cannon. The rear gunner also served as radio operator for the aircraft. Two 23mm/0.9in cannon were fixed in the nose for front defence.

TOP: **Now a museum piece, the Il-28 was a groundbreaking addition to the Soviet inventory – the USSR's first jet bomber.** ABOVE: **Despite its unchallenging appearance, the Il-28 proved to be a major weapon for the Soviet Union.**

LEFT: **A rare picture of a Chinese-built Il-28, the H-5, in service with the Romanian Air Force.** BELOW: **Wartime German jet aircraft development certainly influenced some aspects of the Il-28 design, such as the engines slung beneath the wing. The prototype was, in fact, powered by engines derived from German Jumos.** BOTTOM: **A flight of "Soviet Canberras".**

Using the bomb bay and external hardpoints, the aircraft could carry up to 3000kg/6603lb of ordnance. Wing-tip fuel tanks gave the aircraft extended range. The Il-28R variant was a tactical reconnaissance version with cameras mounted in the bomb bay, but could also carry out electronic intelligence gathering. The Il-28T was the torpedo bomber in service with the Soviet Navy.

The Beagle was retired from the Soviet Air Force and Navy front line in the 1980s but continued to serve as target tugs and ECM (electronic countermeasures) platforms – Finland and East Germany operated the dedicated unarmed target-towing version.

The Il-28 was also operated by a number of export customers, having been sold to over 20 countries including Afghanistan, Egypt, Hungary, Iraq, North Korea, Poland and Yemen. Nigeria's controversial use of their six Il-28s against Biafran civilians in 1968 shocked the world.

Many Arab air forces operated the type, and when 50 examples of this very capable bomber arrived in Egypt in the mid-1950s, tensions between Egypt and Israel rose. During the 1956 Suez crisis and subsequent conflicts in 1967 and 1973, Egyptian Il-28s were targeted on the ground before they could be used against Israel.

Earlier, during the 1962 Cuban Missile Crisis, Soviet Il-28s being assembled on Cuba posed enough of a threat to the USA that the aircraft, as well as the notorious missiles, had to be removed.

Over 500 were sold to China, who also licence-built the aircraft – their domestic version, the H-5, remained in front-line service into the late 1990s. Bomber versions continued to be used by former Soviet satellite and client states well into the 1990s.

### Ilyushin Il-28

**First flight:** August 8, 1948

**Power:** Two Klimov 2700kg/5942lb thrust VK-1 turbojets

**Armament:** Two 23mm/0.9in cannon in nose and two in tail turret; maximum bomb load of 3000kg/6603lb carried internally and externally

**Size:** Wingspan – 21.45m/70ft 4.5in
Length – 17.65m/57ft 10.75in
Height – 6.7m/21ft 11.8in
Wing area – 60.8m²/654.47sq ft

**Weights:** Empty – 12,890kg/28,569lb
Maximum take-off – 21,000kg/46,221lb

**Performance:** Maximum speed – 900kph/559mph
Ceiling – 12,300m/40,355ft
Range – 2180km/1355 miles
Climb – 900m/2953ft per minute

# Lockheed P2V Neptune

Even before the USA entered World War II, it was clear that the US Navy would need a land-based patrol bomber with better performance and armament than the types then available, such as the Hudson and Ventura. The Navy needed an aircraft designed specifically for day or night anti-submarine warfare and anti-shipping operations. Lockheed began work on designing such an aircraft before the Navy managed to issue an official requirement. In the confusion following America's joining the war, the US Navy was only interested in proven and available aircraft types, so Lockheed continued to develop their design with no official support. However, by early 1943 the Navy began to look for the next generation of maritime patrol aircraft and asked Lockheed to proceed to prototype stage. The XP2V-1 first flew on May 17, 1945, and was followed by 14 production versions of the P2V-1, which began to enter US Navy service in March 1947. The designers introduced many production refinements with the aircraft, for example trying to keep much of the fuselage shape curving in only one direction, thus allowing the use of shaped skins which would fit in any number of areas on the fuselage instead of just one. The aircraft was designed to be

RIGHT: **Test-flown during World War II, the Neptune was finally retired from active duty four decades later. The aircraft pictured here is a Dutch Navy machine.** BELOW: **An excellent air-to-air study of a US Navy P2V. Note the remotely controlled searchlight on the tip of the starboard wingtip fuel tank.**

manufactured into easily accessible subassemblies, keeping assembly time to a minimum. The Neptune thus became an easy aircraft to service – for example, a complete engine change could be done in 30 minutes and an outer wing panel in 79 minutes.

However, the Neptune had made a name for itself before it entered service. From September to October 1946, a modified Neptune named Truculent Turtle flew 18,100km/11,250 miles non-stop from Western Australia to Columbus, Ohio, in 55 hours and 15 minutes, and captured the world long-distance record.

Over 30 variants of the P2V appeared before production ceased in 1962. After the P2V-1, the improved and more powerfully engined P2V-2, with the ability to carry sonobuoys, was the next significant version. However, the major production version was the P2V-5, first flown on December 29, 1950.

Powered by 3250hp R-3350 engines, this version carried additional fuel in ingenious large wingtip tanks. Apart from 1589 litres/350 gallons of fuel, the forward portion of the starboard wingtip tank housed a powerful moveable searchlight that was linked to the movement of the nose turret guns. The port wingtip tank had APS-8 search radar mounted in its forward portion, and both tanks could be jettisoned in an emergency. The P2V-5 could carry a 3632kg/8000lb bomb load of mines, torpedoes, bombs or depth charges, as well as 16 rockets beneath the wings. An APS-20 radar was mounted in the underbelly position just aft of the nose-wheel doors. The increase in ASW and ECM (electronic countermeasures equipment) required an increase in the aircrew to nine men, and the P2V-5's range was 7642km/4750 miles.

In addition to the US Navy, the P2V-5 was supplied to Argentina, Australia, Brazil, the Netherlands and Portugal. Fifty-two P2V-5s were delivered to the Royal Air Force in 1952. Designated Neptune MR.1s, the aircraft were delivered with nose, dorsal and tail turrets. Twenty-seven were later modified, and the nose and tail turrets replaced with the clear plexiglass nose and MAD boom in the tail. The Neptune entered service with No.217 Squadron and also equipped Nos.36, 203 and 210 Squadrons. The aircraft were returned to the USA in 1957 when the RAF's Shackleton force was up to strength.

The P2V-7 was the final Neptune version off the production line. First flown on April 26, 1954, it was powered by two piston engines augmented by two turbojets. With a dash speed of 586kph/364mph, this version was the fastest of the Lockheed-produced Neptunes. The APS-20 search radar, with its larger radome, was mounted further forward than on the P2V-5s.

By the 1970s, P2Vs had been phased out from all US Navy Fleet Patrol Squadrons but remained in service with Reserve Patrol Squadrons. In April 1978, the last reserve unit re-equipped with the P-3 Orion, thus ending over three decades of P2V Neptune operations with the US Navy.

Kawasaki had assembled some 48 P2V-7s in Japan and went on to produce a developed turboprop-powered version, designated P-2J, with a longer fuselage to carry more equipment. The turboprops were again augmented by two turbojets. A total of 83 P-2Js were built by Kawasaki, with the first delivered in October 1969. These aircraft, the last operational Neptunes in the world, were finally retired in 1985.

TOP: **A P2V-7 of French Aéronavale unit Escadrille 12S.** TOP RIGHT: **A Dutch Navy Neptune.** ABOVE: **An RAF crew gaining experience of one of 50 P2V-5 Neptunes allocated to Britain and Australia before flying the aircraft to the UK.**

### Lockheed P2V-7 Neptune

**First Flight:** May 17, 1945 (XP2V-1 prototype)

**Power:** Two Wright 3500hp R-3350-32W radial piston engines and two Westinghouse 1543kg/3400lb thrust J34-WE-36 turbojets

**Armament:** Two 12.7mm/0.5in machine-guns in dorsal turret; up to 3632kg/8000lb of bombs, depth charges or torpedoes

**Size:** Wingspan – 31.65m/103ft 10in
Length – 27.94m/91ft 8in
Height – 8.94m/29ft 4in
Wing area – 92.9m²/1000sq ft

**Weights:** Empty – 22,670kg/49,935lb
Maximum take-off – 36,272kg/79,895lb

**Performance:** Maximum speed – 649kph/403mph
Ceiling – 6710m/22,000ft
Range – 5930km/3685 miles
Climb – 366m/1200ft per minute

# Lockheed P-3 Orion

The P-3C Orion is one of the all-time great military aircraft. Developed quickly in a time of national need from the existing Lockheed Electra airliner, the Orion has been protecting the maritime interests of the USA and other P-3 customers for over four decades, and remains a potent submarine killer.

In 1957, the US Navy issued an urgent requirement for a long-range maritime reconnaissance and anti-submarine warfare (ASW) aircraft to replace the ageing P2V Neptune. Lockheed's answer was a modified Electra airliner airframe, which first flew in November 1959. Structurally, the aircraft differed in that the Orion was 2.24m/7ft 4in shorter and had a weapons bay for carrying mines, torpedoes, depth charges or even nuclear weapons.

The aircraft entered the US Navy inventory in July 1962, and more than 30 years later it remains the Navy's sole land-based ASW aircraft. It has gone through one designation change (P3V to P-3) and three major models – P-3A, P-3B and P-3C, the latter being the only one now in active service. The last Navy P-3 came off the Lockheed production line in April 1990.

The P-3 Orion built its reputation as the ultimate submarine-finder during the Cold War. From the Cuban Missile Crisis to the end of the Soviet Union, the Orion carried out round-the-clock, low-profile patrols to keep the USA and NATO ahead of the Soviets.

The P-3 can be equipped with a variety of sophisticated detection equipment. Infrared and long-range electro-optical cameras plus special imaging radar allow the Orion, with no

TOP: **The P-3 is still among the best ASW aircraft in the world, almost half a century after its first flight.** ABOVE: **A Royal Netherlands Navy P-3.**

defensive armament, to monitor activity from a safe distance. It can stay airborne for very long periods, and its four powerful Allison T56-A-14 engines can fly at almost any altitude.

In addition to submarine-hunting, the P-3 is called upon for peacekeeping and relief missions around the world. When civil war flared in Liberia, P-3s were the eyes and ears of forces protecting the US Embassy. In Somalia, P-3s monitored street operations in Mogadishu from well off-shore. In Rwanda, P-3s tracked large groups of refugees to help pinpoint relief efforts. Then, in Operation Desert Storm, P-3s logged more than 12,000 hours in 1200 combat surveillance sorties.

The current US Navy force of 12 active and seven reserve squadrons supports requirements for 40 P-3Cs to be continuously forward-deployed around the world, ready

RIGHT: **The US Navy will continue to operate P-3s for some years to come. This aircraft has opened the doors of its weapons bay, which can contain torpedoes, nuclear depth charges and mines.** BELOW: **This photograph of a US Navy P-3 shows the area beneath the fuselage aft of the wing, consisting of over 50 chutes from which a variety of stores can be dispensed.** BELOW RIGHT: **The P-3 has now become a battlefield surveillance platform over land and sea.**

to support global US Navy operations. In addition to US Navy use, P-3s were exported to Australia, Chile, Greece, Iran, the Netherlands, New Zealand, Norway, Portugal, South Korea, Spain and Thailand. Some were also built in Japan by Kawasaki, and the Canadian Armed Forces operate a version known as the CP-140 Aurora.

US Navy P-3s were active in Afghanistan in late 2001, where the aircraft used data links to provide real-time video and other sensor data to land forces.

The role of the Orion has evolved from being simply a maritime anti-submarine aircraft to being a battlefield surveillance platform at sea or over land. The aircraft's long range and loiter time proved to be invaluable assets for the Allies during Operation Iraqi Freedom because it can view the battle area and instantaneously provide that information to ground troops.

The P-3C has advanced submarine-detection sensors such as directional frequency and ranging (DIFAR) sonobuoys and magnetic anomaly detection (MAD) equipment. The avionics system is integrated by a computer that supports all of the tactical displays and monitors for the 11 crew members, and can automatically launch weapons, as well as providing flight information to the pilots. The aircraft can carry a variety of weapons internally and on wing pylons, such as the Harpoon anti-surface missile, the Mk 50 torpedo and the Mk 60 mine. From the Cold War to today's tensions, the P-3 was there, and it is likely to remain in service around the world for the foreseeable future.

## Lockheed Martin P-3C Orion

**First Flight** November 25, 1959 (YP-3A)
**Power** Four Allison 4910eshp T-56-A-14 turboprop engines
**Armament** 9080kg/20,000lb of ordnance, including cruise missile, Maverick (AGM 65) air-to-ground missiles, Mk 46/50 torpedoes, rockets, mines, depth bombs and special weapons
**Size** Wingspan – 30.36m/99ft 6in
Length – 35.6m/116ft 10in
Height – 10.27m/33ft 7in
Wing area – 120.77m²/1300sq ft
**Weights** Empty – 27,917kg/61,491lb
Maximum take-off – 64,468kg/142,000lb
**Performance** Maximum speed – 750kph/466mph
Ceiling – 8631m/28,300ft
Range – 4405km/2738 miles
Climb – 594m/1950ft per minute

# Lockheed S-3 Viking

The S-3 Viking in service today is an all-weather, carrier-based patrol/attack aircraft, which provides protection for the US fleet against hostile surface vessels while also functioning as the Carrier Battle Groups' primary tanker. The S-3, one of the most successful of all carrier aircraft, is extremely versatile and is equipped for many missions, including day/night surveillance, electronic countermeasures, command/control/communications warfare, as well as search-and-rescue (SAR). Its versatility has made it known as the "Swiss Army Knife of Naval Aviation".

In the late 1960s, the deployment of Soviet deep-diving nuclear powered submarines caused the US Navy to call for a new breed of carrier-borne US Navy ASW aircraft to succeed the Grumman S-2. Lockheed, in association with Vought Aeronautics, proposed the S-3A, which came to be called Viking.

To keep the aircraft aerodynamically clean and avoid reducing its top speed, as many protuberances as possible were designed to retract. Thus, the inflight refuelling probe, the magnetic anomaly detection boom at the rear of the aircraft and some sensors retract for transit flight. The small four-man aircraft has folding wings, making it very popular on carriers due to the small amount of space it takes up relative to the importance of its mission. With its short, stubby wings, the Viking was something of a wolf in sheep's clothing and could have given a very good account of itself had the Cold War heated up. Carrying state-of-the-art radar

TOP: **Developed to counter a specific Soviet threat, the Viking is considered to be the ultimate sub-killer.** ABOVE: **An S-3B of VS-31 "Topcats" aboard the USS *John F. Kennedy*, Arabian Sea, April 2004.**

systems and extensive sonobuoy deployment and control capability, the S-3A entered US Navy service with VS-41 in February 1974. In total 187 were built and equipped 14 US Navy squadrons.

In the mid-1980s, the aircraft was completely refurbished and modified to carry the Harpoon missile, the improved version being designated the S-3B. While the S-3A was primarily configured for anti-submarine warfare, the S-3B has evolved into a premier surveillance and precision-targeting platform for the US Navy, and has the most modern precision-guided missile capabilities. It does so many things so well – surface and undersea warfare, mine warfare, electronic reconnaissance and analysis, over-the-horizon targeting, missile attack, and aerial tanking – that its current mission is summed up by the US Navy as being simply "Sea Control".

ABOVE: **The Viking has an internal weapons bay which can carry bombs, depth charges, mines and torpedoes, while missiles, rocket pods, bombs, flare dispensers or mines can be carried on two underwing hardpoints.**

The S-3B's high-speed computer system processes and displays information generated by its targeting-sensor systems. To engage and destroy targets, the S-3B Viking employs an impressive array of airborne weaponry, including the AGM 84 Harpoon Anti-Ship Missile, AGM 65 Maverick Infrared Missile and a wide selection of conventional bombs and torpedoes. Future Viking aircraft will also have a control capability for the AGM 84 stand-off land-attack missile extended range (SLAM-ER). The S-3B provides the fleet with a very effective fixed-wing "over the horizon" aircraft to combat the significant and varied threats presented by modern maritime combatants.

On March 25, 2003, an S-3B from the "Red Griffins" of Sea Control Squadron Thirty-eight (VS 38) became the first such aircraft to attack inland and to fire a laser-guided Maverick missile in combat. The attack was made on a "significant naval target" in the Tigris River near Basra, Iraq. VS-38 was embarked in the USS *Constellation*.

The Viking, easy to update with the latest avionics and surveillance equipment, will be flying with the US Navy for many years to come.

TOP: **The aircraft carries a long magnetic anomaly detection boom which can be extended from the rear of the aircraft to aid submarine-detection.**
ABOVE: **An S-3A of VS-22 "The Checkmates" from USS *Saratoga*.**
BELOW: **The S-3B's mission, neatly summed up by the US Navy, is "Sea Control".**

## Lockheed S-3B Viking

**First Flight** January 21, 1972
**Power** Two General Electric 4211kg/9275lb thrust TF-34-GE-400B turbofan engines
**Armament** Up to 1793kg/3950lb of ordnance, including AGM-84 Harpoon, AGM-65 Maverick and AGM-84 SLAM missiles, torpedoes, rockets and bombs
**Size:** Wingspan – 20.93m/68ft 8in
  Length – 16.26m/53ft 4in
  Height – 6.93m/22ft 9in
  Wing area – 55.55m²/598sq ft
**Weights** Empty – 12,099kg/26,650lb
  Maximum take-off – 23,852kg/52,539lb
**Performance** Maximum speed – 834kph/518mph
  Ceiling – 12,200m/40,000ft
  Range – 3706km/2303 miles
  Climb – 1280m/4200ft per minute

# Lockheed Martin F-117A Nighthawk

Usually and erroneously referred to as the "stealth fighter", the F-117A Nighthawk bomber was the world's first operational aircraft designed to exploit low-observability stealth technology. This precision-strike aircraft can penetrate high-threat airspace undetected and then use laser-guided weaponry against critical targets.

The F-117A was developed by Lockheed Martin after lengthy work on stealth technology was carried out in secret from 1975. Development of the F-117A began in 1978, and it

TOP: **Developed in incredible secrecy, the "stealth fighter" was the world's first operational aircraft built with stealth technology.** ABOVE: **Braking parachutes trailing, a pair of F-117As during a visit to the UK.**

was test-flown in 1981, but it was not until 1988 that its existence was publicly announced. The first F-117A was delivered in 1982, and USAF Air Combat Command's first F-117A unit, the 4450th Tactical Group, achieved operational capability in October 1983. Lockheed Martin delivered the last of 59 aircraft to the Air Force in July 1990, and five additional test aircraft were retained by the company.

The aircraft's surfaces and edge profiles are optimized to reflect hostile radar into narrow beam signals, directed away from enemy radar detectors. All the doors and opening panels on the aircraft have saw-toothed forward and trailing edges to reflect radar. The aircraft is constructed principally of aluminum, with titanium used for areas of the engine and exhaust systems. The outer surface of the aircraft is coated with a radar-absorbent material (RAM) and for stealth reasons, the F-117A does not rely on radar for navigation or targeting. Instead, for navigation and weapon aiming, the aircraft is equipped with a forward-looking infrared (FLIR) and a downward-looking infrared (DLIR) with laser designator, supplied by Raytheon.

The F-117A is powered by two low-bypass General Electric F404-GE-F1D2 turbofan engines. The rectangular air intakes on both sides of the fuselage are covered by gratings that are coated with radar-absorbent material. The wide and flat structure of the engine exhaust area reduces the infrared and radar detectability of the aft section of the engine. The two large tail fins slant slightly outwards to provide an obstruction for ground-based radars to the infrared and radar returns from the engine exhaust area.

Before a flight, mission data is downloaded on to the IBM AP-102 mission-control computer, which integrates it with the navigation and flight controls to provide a fully automated flight management system. After take-off, the pilot can hand over flight control to the mission programme until within visual range of the mission's first target. The pilot then resumes control of the aircraft for weapon delivery. The aircraft is equipped with an infrared acquisition and designation system (IRADS), which is integrated with the weapon delivery system. The pilot is presented with a view of the target on the head-up display. After the strike, the weapon delivery and impact is recorded on the aircraft's internally-mounted video system, which provides real-time damage assessment.

The F-117A can employ a variety of weapons, including the BLU-109B low-level laser-guided bomb, GBU-10 and GBU-27 laser-guided bomb units, AGM-65 Maverick and AGM-88 HARM air-to-surface missiles.

The F-117A first saw action in December 1989 during Operation Just Cause in Panama, but it was the type's actions in the first Gulf War that grabbed the headlines. On their first trip into theatre, the F-117s flew non-stop from the USA to Kuwait, an air-refuelled flight of approximately 18.5 hours – a record for single-seat combat aircraft that stands today.

In January and February 1991, the F-117A attacked the most heavily fortified targets during Desert Storm, and it was the only coalition jet allowed to strike targets inside Baghdad's

RIGHT: **The principal weapon carried by the F-117 is the precision laser-guided GBU-27 bomb.** BELOW: **The F-117, with its unprecedented form, was so radical that it has challenged how we think combat aircraft should look.**

city limits. The F-117A, which normally packs a payload of two 908kg/2000lb GBU-27 laser-guided bombs, destroyed and crippled Iraqi electrical power stations, military headquarters, communications sites, air-defence operation centres, airfields, ammunition bunkers and chemical, biological and nuclear weapons plants.

Although only 36 F-117As were deployed in Desert Storm, and accounted for 2.5 per cent of the total force of 1900 fighters and bombers, they flew more than a third of the bombing runs on the first day of the war. In all, during Desert Storm this remarkable aircraft conducted more than 1250 sorties, dropped more than 2032 tonnes/2000 tons of bombs, and flew for more than 6900 hours. Although more than 3000 anti-aircraft guns and 60 surface-to-air missile batteries protected Baghdad, the Nighthawks owned the skies over the city and, for that matter, the country.

In March 24, 1999, F-117As led the NATO Operation Allied Force air strikes against Yugoslavia. During the campaign, one F-117 was lost, having being tracked by virtually antique Russian long wavelength radars. Normally the only time the aircraft's stealthiness can be compromised is when it gets very wet or opens its bomb bays.

Nighthawks are officially expected to remain in USAF service until 2020, but with updating, the aircraft is likely to be around for much longer.

**Lockheed Martin
F-117A Nighthawk**

**First Flight:** June 18, 1981
**Power:** Two General Electric 4903kg/10,800lb
thrust F404-GE-F1D2 non-afterburning turbofans
**Armament:** Up to 2270kg/5000lb of smart or
free-fall weapons can be carried internally
**Size:** Wingspan – 13.3m/43ft 4in
Length – 20.1m/65ft 11in
Height – 3.78m/12ft 5in
Wing area – 105.9m²/1140sq ft
**Weights:** Empty – Approximately 13,620kg/30,000lb
Maximum take-off – 23,835kg/52,500lb
**Performance:** Maximum speed – High subsonic
Ceiling – Unpublished
Range – Intercontinental with air-refuelling
Climb – Unpublished

**91**

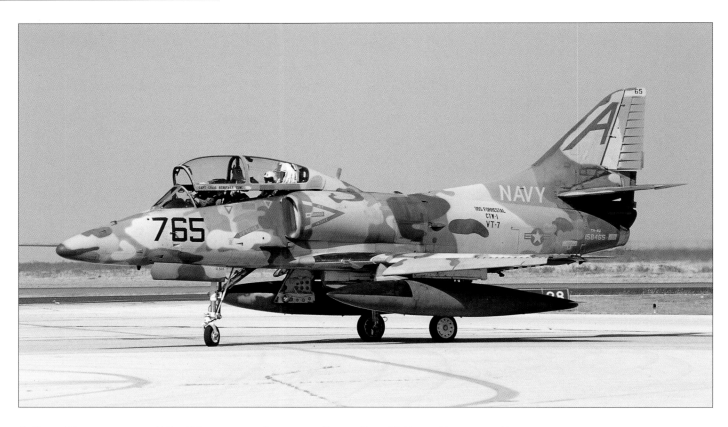

# McDonnell Douglas A-4 Skyhawk

From 1954, Douglas (and later McDonnell Douglas) built 2960 Skyhawks in a production run that lasted a quarter of a century. Designed as a small and therefore cost-effective lightweight carrier-borne high-speed bomber, the Skyhawk was affectionately nicknamed "the scooter" or "Heinemann's Hot Rod" after Douglas designer Ed Heinemann. He had been working on a compact jet-powered attack aircraft design which the US Navy ordered for evaluation – this was the XA4D-1, and the first of nine prototypes and development aircraft flew in June 1954. Development was swift and the Navy were eager to acquire this new and very capable combat aircraft. Chosen as a replacement for the venerable Skyraider,

the Skyhawk provided the US Navy, US Marines Corps and friendly nations with a manoeuvrable but powerful attack bomber that had great altitude and range performance, plus a remarkable and flexible weapons-carrying capability.

Production deliveries of A-4As began in September 1956. The A-4 was first delivered to the US Navy's VA-72 attack squadron on October 26, 1956. Its small size allowed it to fit on an aircraft carrier lift without needing to have folding wings, thus saving weight and extra maintenance. The Skyhawk was roughly half the empty weight of its contemporaries and could fly at 1089km/677mph at sea level. US examples of the aircraft were nuclear-capable.

The Skyhawk was progressively developed with more powerful engines – early A–C models had been powered by the Wright J65, a licence-built copy of the British Armstrong Siddeley Sapphire engine. The A-4C was followed by the A-4E, a heavier aircraft powered by Pratt & Whitney's J52 engine. The A-4F was the last version to enter US Navy service and was easily identified by its dorsal avionics "hump". The ultimate development of the Skyhawk was the A-4M, known as the Skyhawk II, specifically designed for the US Marines. This model that first flew in 1970 had a larger canopy for better pilot view, and had a maximum take-off

LEFT: The A-4D2 version had a more efficient engine, beefed-up rear fuselage and powered rudder, and introduced the fixed inflight refuelling probe. BELOW: The "camel's hump", which appeared on later A-4s, housed all-weather navigation and weapons-delivery avionics. BOTTOM: Two-seat trainer versions of the A-4 were produced to train both pilots and radar intercept officers.

weight twice that of the early A-4 versions. Power for this "super" Skyhawk came from a J52-P-408, and the Skyhawk II was in production until 1979. The US Navy's Blue Angels flight demonstration aerobatics team flew the A-4 Skyhawk II from 1974 until 1986.

The Skyhawk's combat career began on August 4, 1964, with the first American carrier-launched raids on North Vietnam. The A-4s were soon performing most of the Navy's and Marine Corps' light air attack missions over Vietnam.

Skyhawks were also operated by the armed forces of Argentina, Australia, Israel (who used them extensively in the 1973 Yom Kippur war), Kuwait, Singapore, Indonesia, Malaysia and New Zealand, and they remained active with several air services into the 2000s.

Argentina was the first export customer for the Skyhawk, operating A-4Ps and A-4Qs which were modified B and C-models respectively. These aircraft, acquired in the mid-1960s, were later complemented by A-4Rs which were ex-USMC A-4Ms. Argentine Skyhawks were the most

destructive strike aircraft to engage British Forces during the 1982 Falklands War. Operating from mainland bases, the Skyhawks carried out many attacks against British shipping. On May 12, a Skyhawk raid put HMS Glasgow out of action, and on May 21, the Skyhawks attacked the British invasion force landing at San Carlos. On May 25, Argentine Skyhawks attacked and sank HMS Coventry. The cost of these actions was high, with Argentina losing ten A-4s to anti-aircraft defences and fighters in a matter of days.

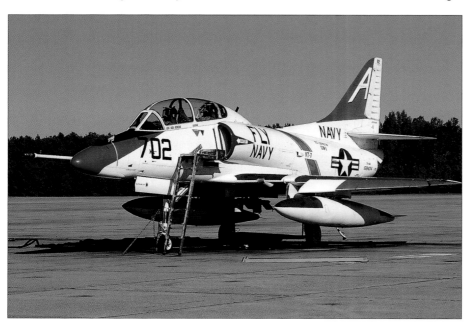

## McDonnell Douglas A-4M Skyhawk II

**First flight:** June 22, 1954 (XA4D-1 prototype)
**Power:** One Pratt & Whitney 5079kg/11,187lb thrust J52-P408 turbojet
**Armament:** Two 20mm/0.78in cannon in wing roots; up to 4156kg/9155lb of bombs or air-to-surface and air-to-air missiles
**Size** Wingspan – 8.38m/27ft 6in
Length – 12.27m/40ft 4in
Height – 4.5m/15ft
Wing area – 24.2m²/260sq ft
**Weights:** Empty – 4751kg/10,465lb
Maximum take-off – 11,123kg/24,500lb
**Performance:** Maximum speed – 1100kph/683mph
Ceiling – 11803m/38,700ft
Range – 1480km/920 miles
Climb – 3142m/10,300ft per minute

# McDonnell Douglas F-4 Phantom II

The F-4, one of the world's greatest-ever combat aircraft, was designed to meet a US Navy requirement for a fleet defence fighter to replace the F3H Demon and to counter the threat from long-range Soviet bombers. The US Air Force also ordered the Phantom when the F-4 was shown to be faster than their high-performance F-104. The F-4 was first used by the US Navy as an interceptor, but was soon employed by the US Marine Corps in the ground support role. Its outstanding versatility made it the first US multi-service aircraft to fly with the US Air Force, Navy and Marine Corps concurrently. The remarkable Phantom excelled in air superiority, close air support, interception, air defence suppression, long-range strike, fleet defence, attack and reconnaissance.

The sophisticated F-4 was, without direction from surface-based radar, able to detect and destroy a target beyond visual range (BVR). In the Vietnam and Gulf Wars alone, the F-4 was credited with 280 air-to-air victories. As a bomber, the F-4 could carry up to 5.08 tonnes/5 tons of ordnance and deliver it accurately while flying at supersonic speeds at very low level.

Capable of flying at twice the speed of sound with ease, the Phantom was loved by its crews, who considered it a workhorse that could be relied on, that could do the job and get them home safely. F-4s have also set world records for altitude (30,059m/98,556ft on December 6, 1959), speed (2585kph/1606mph on November 22, 1961) and a low-altitude speed record of 1452kph/902mph that stood for 16 years.

Phantom production ran from 1958 to 1979, resulting in a total of 5195 aircraft. Of these, 5057 were made in St Louis,

TOP: **The F-4, a jack of all trades and master of them all, is considered by many to be the greatest ever combat aircraft. This photograph shows an F-4G optimized to neutralize hostile radars.** ABOVE: **Germany's F-4F fleet will remain in service until 2015.**

Missouri, in the USA, while a further 138 were built under licence by the Mitsubishi Aircraft Co. in Japan. F-4 production peaked in 1967 when the McDonnell plant was producing 72 Phantoms per month. The USAF acquired 2874 while the US Navy and Marine Corps operated 1264.

The F-4 was used extensively by the USA in Vietnam from 1965 and served in many roles including fighter, reconnaissance and ground attack. A number of refurbished ex-US forces

ABOVE: **An F-4E releases its bombs.** RIGHT: **The F-4 has set world records for speed and altitude.** BELOW: **The Phantom has served both the Royal Air Force and the Royal Navy. Britain retired its last Phantom in 1992.**

aircraft were operated by other nations, including the UK, who bought a squadron of mothballed ex-US Navy F-4Js to complement the RAF's F-4Ms.

Regularly updated with the addition of state-of-the-art weaponry and radar, the Phantom served with 11 nations around the globe – Australia, Egypt, Germany, Greece, Iran, Israel, Japan, South Korea, Spain and Turkey. Britain's Royal Navy and Royal Air Force both operated Phantoms from 1968, and the last RAF Phantoms were retired in January 1992. For a time, RAF F.G.R.2 Phantoms with the ability to carry 11 454kg/1000lb bombs were based in Germany in the tactical nuclear bomber role.

1996 saw the Phantom's retirement from US military forces, by which time the type had flown more than 27,350,000km/ around 17 million miles in the nation's service. Israel, Japan, Germany, Turkey, Greece, Korea and Egypt have undertaken or plan to upgrade their F-4s and keep them flying until 2015, nearly 60 years after the Phantom's first flight.

### McDonnell Douglas Phantom F.G.R.2 (F-4M)

**First flight:** February 17, 1967

**Power:** Two Rolls-Royce 9313kg/20,515lb afterburning thrust Spey 202 turbofans

**Armament:** One 20mm/0.78in cannon; eleven 454kg/1000lb free-fall or retarded conventional or nuclear bombs, 126 68mm/ 2.65in armour-piercing rockets, all carried externally

**Size:** Wingspan – 11.68m/38ft 4in
Length – 17.73m/58ft 2in
Height – 4.95m/16ft 3in
Wing area – 49.25m²/530sq ft

**Weights** Empty – 14,074kg/31,000lb
Maximum take-off – 26,332kg/58,000lb

**Performance:** Maximum speed – 2230kph/ 1386mph
Ceiling – 18,300m/60,000ft
Range – 2815km/1750 miles
Climb – 9760m/32,000ft per minute

# McDonnell Douglas/Boeing F-15

The F-15 Eagle, designed to succeed the legendary F-4 Phantom, is a highly manoeuvrable, all-weather combat aircraft originally designed to gain and maintain US Air Force air superiority in aerial combat. It is probably the most capable multi-role fighter in service today.

The first F-15A flight was made in July 1972, and the test-flight of the two-seat F-15B trainer was made in July 1973. The first USAF Eagle (an F-15B) was delivered to the US Air Force in November 1974, while the first Eagle destined for a front-line combat squadron was delivered in January 1976, and some squadrons were combat-ready by the end of the year.

In the fighter role the Eagle's air superiority is achieved through a mixture of incredible manoeuvrability and acceleration, range, weapons and avionics, and in the strike role it can penetrate enemy defences and outperform and outfight any current potential enemy aircraft. The F-15's manoeuvrability and acceleration are due to its high engine thrust-to-weight ratio and low wing-loading. Low wing-loading (the ratio of aircraft weight to its wing area) is a vital factor in manoeuvrability and, combined with the high thrust-to-weight ratio, enables the aircraft to turn tightly without losing airspeed in the process.

The F-15E Strike Eagle, which first flew in July 1980, is a two-seat, dual-role fighter for all-weather, air-to-air and deep interdiction missions – the rear cockpit is reserved for the weapon systems operator (WSO) and incorporates an entirely new suite of air-to-ground avionics. On four television-like screens, the WSO can display information from the radar, electronic warfare or infrared sensors, monitor aircraft or weapon status and possible threats, select targets, and use an electronic "moving map" to navigate. Two hand controls are used to select new displays and to refine targeting information. Displays can be moved from one screen to another, chosen from a "menu" of display options.

While earlier models of the Eagle were purely air-to-air combat aircraft, the E-model is a dual-role fighter. It can fight its way to a target over long ranges, destroy enemy ground positions, and fight its way back out. The F-15E performs day

TOP: **Preparing to land, with massive dorsal airbrake extended, this Israeli F-15 shows some of the weapon-carrying ability of the type.** ABOVE: **An F-15E Strike Eagle of the 48th TFW based at Lakenheath, UK.**

and night all-weather air-to-air and air-to-ground missions including strategic strike. Its engines incorporate advanced digital technology for improved performance, and acceleration from a standstill to maximum afterburner takes less than four seconds. Although primarily a bomber, the F-15E is equally at home performing fighter and escort missions.

The F-15E became the newest fighter in USAF Tactical Air Command when the 405th Tactical Training Wing accepted delivery of the first production model in April 1988. Strike Eagles were among the first US aircraft in action during the first Gulf War, and they spearheaded an attack on Iraqi forces on January 16, 1991.

The F-15E can carry an external payload of up to 11,123kg/ 24,500lb, including fuel tanks, missiles and bombs. Considered to be the most advanced tactical fighter aircraft in the world, the F-15E is the fifth version of the F-15 to appear since 1972.

More than 1500 F-15s have been produced for the USA and international customers Israel, Japan and Saudi Arabia. The F-15I Thunder, a strike version designed for Israel, was built in the USA, the first of 25 Thunders arriving in Israel in January 1998.

TOP: **The dual-role Strike Eagle can battle its way to a target like a fighter, and then carry out a devastating bombing attack.** ABOVE: **The Strike Eagle was designed to succeed the long range F-111.** LEFT: **The F-15 can operate in all weather, day or night.** BELOW: **Fighter escort or strike missions – both are specialities of the F-15E.**

### McDonnell Douglas F-15E

**First flight:** July 27, 1972
**Power:** Two Pratt & Whitney 13,211kg/ 29,100lb afterburning thrust F100-PW-229 turbofans
**Armament:** One 20mm/0.78in cannon; 11,123kg/ 24,500lb of external store, including free-fall, retarded, guided, nuclear or conventional bombs, as well as missiles
**Size:** Wingspan – 13.04m/42ft 9.5in
Length – 19.44m/63ft 9.5in
Height – 5.64m/18ft 6in
Wing area – 56.48m²/608sq ft
**Weights:** Empty – 14,528kg/32,000lb
Maximum take-off – 36,774kg/81,000lb
**Performance:** Maximum speed – 2655kph/ 1650mph
Ceiling – 19,215m/63,000ft
Range – 4445km/2760 miles
Climb – 15,250m/50,000ft per minute

# Mikoyan-Gurevich MiG-27

The MiG-21's range never lived up to expectations, and led to a 1965 requirement for a replacement with considerably better endurance. An enlarged MiG-21 and the all-new Ye-23-11/1 were proposed, the latter becoming the prototype MiG-23 which first appeared in 1967. Like the MiG-21, the new aircraft was proposed in two versions – an interceptor for use with Russia's PVO air defence forces and a ground-attack version, the MiG-27, to serve with Russia's tactical air forces, Frontal Aviation.

The MiG-23 was not only Russia's first production aircraft with a variable-geometry "swing wing"; it was also the first swing-wing fighter anywhere. It and the MiG-27 have three sweep positions: minimum (16 degrees) for take-off, low-speed flight and landing; middle (45 degrees) for cruising; and maximum (72 degrees) for high-performance flight. The aircraft's swing wings are high-mounted, and the single engine is fed by rectangular box-like air intakes forward of the wing roots.

The MiG-27 is an improved but simplified version of the close air-support and ground-attack MiG-23, designed to fly at a slower speed and lower altitude, carrying a larger weapon load with better radar and precision missile-aiming equipment. The MiG-27 (known to NATO as Flogger-D) can be distinguished from the MiG-23 by a different nose (housing a laser rangefinder and other sensors) which slopes away sharply from the cockpit for better pilot view, earning the nickname "Ducknose" from its crews. The MiG-27 pilot is seated higher for better visibility, and the nose has a flattened glass underside, which contains the TV tracker unit and laser rangefinder/designator.

The MiG's multi-barrel GSh-6-N-30 30mm/1.18in autocannon has been likened to the A-10's Vulcan cannon, and is a very potent ground-attack weapon which can spew out 900 rounds of 30mm/1.18in shells over an effective range of 2000m/6562ft.

Due to its role as a battlefield attack aircraft, the pilot of the MiG-27 is protected from small-arms fire by armour on the side of the cockpit. Terrain-avoidance radar relieves the pilot of some of the high workload associated with low-level operations. The MiG-27 lacks the MiG-23's air-to-air radar, relying instead on fighter cover over the battlefield to perform its mission. It also has a different engine, different landing gear, and a navigation/attack system tailored to the ground-attack mission in all weathers. The carriage of various reconnaissance pods means that the aircraft can carry out tactical reconnaissance missions. The MiG-27 has reportedly also been operated from Soviet aircraft carriers.

ABOVE: **The last of the line, an Indian-manufactured MiG-27M Flogger in Indian Air Force service.** LEFT: **Note the rocket pods on this Czechoslovakian Air Force machine.**

LEFT: **Although some MiG-27s have become museum exhibits, the type remains in front-line use with many nations.** BELOW: **The MiG-23/27 was the Soviet Union's first variable-geometry aircraft.** BOTTOM: **Indian-built Floggers are known as Bahadur (Valiant).**

Among the operators of the MiG-23/-27 were Poland, Hungary, Bulgaria, East Germany, Romania and Czechoslovakia. Downgraded MiG-23s were exported outside the Warsaw Pact nations to Libya, Syria, Egypt, Ethiopia, India, Cuba, Algeria, Iraq, Afghanistan and North Korea. Russian MiG-27 production was completed in the mid-1980s, but India's Hindustan Aeronautics produced MiG-27Ms (locally named Bahadur or Valiant) for the Indian Air Force until 1997, finally bringing Flogger production to a close after nearly three decades, with around 4000 examples built.

MiG-27s were used in combat in Afghanistan by the Soviets from 1979 until 1989. Iraqi machines were used in the Iran-Iraq War between 1980 and 1988, and again briefly during the Gulf War of 1991.

## Mikoyan-Gurevich MiG-27

**First flight:** 1972
**Power:** One Tumansky 11,500kg/25,311lb afterburning thrust R-29B-300 turbojet
**Armament:** One 30mm/1.18in cannon in belly; seven pylons for carrying up to 4000kg/8804lb of ordnance, including air-to-air missiles, Kh-29 air-to-surface missiles, AS-7 "Kerry" air-to-surface missiles, rockets and napalm tanks, conventional or tactical nuclear bombs
**Size:** Wingspan – 13.97m/45ft 10in, spread
Length – 17.08m/56ft
Height – 5m/16ft 5in
Wing area – 37.4m²/402.1sq ft
**Weights:** Empty – 11,910kg/26,214lb
Maximum take-off – 20,300kg/44,680lb
**Performance:** Maximum speed – 1885kph/1170mph
Ceiling – 14,008m/45,960ft
Range – 1080km/670 miles
Climb – 12,007m/39,395ft per minute

# Myasishchev M-4

Development of a Soviet intercontinental bomber capable of striking US-territory began in the early 1950s. In March 1951, a new design bureau led by Vladimir Myasishchev was established to organize the development and manufacture of a bomber with a range of up to 12,000km/7452 miles, a maximum speed of 900kph/559mph, and the ability to carry a payload of 5000kg/11,005lb. Myasishchev's response was a swept-wing bomber powered by four jet engines buried in the wing roots. While Tupolev believed that only turboprops could provide the great range required to do the job with their Tu-95, Myasishchev instead opted for turbojets.

The high-power engines needed for the production aircraft were still in development, so the prototype, completed in December 1952, was fitted with four AM-3A turbojet engines developed by Mikulin. The prototype had its first flight on January 20, 1953. It achieved a top speed of 947kph/588mph and an altitude of 12,500m/41,012ft, but failed to achieve the required range. Despite this, production of the M-4 began in Moscow in 1955, and it became the Soviet Union's first operational four-jet strategic bomber. The M-4 made its first public appearance in a fly-past over Moscow on May 1, 1954, and was given the NATO codename "Bison". Features of the aircraft included two main undercarriage units arranged in tandem on the fuselage centreline plus twin-wheel outriggers, which retracted into the wingtips. The nose and tail units of the aircraft were pressurized for crew comfort.

The M-4/2M "Bison A" was the original free-fall nuclear bomber version produced, and can be easily identified by the typical Soviet "greenhouse" glazed nose. Many were later

TOP: **With air-refuelling, the M-4 could have attacked the continental USA from Soviet bases with ease.** ABOVE: **The "Bison" was an enormous aircraft – this aircraft is seen at the July 1967 Aviation Festival at Moscow's Domodedovo Airport.**

converted into tankers by the addition of a hose-reel unit in the bomb bay and were used to extend the range of other M-4s, as well as Tu-95s.

Range was always the issue with the M-4, so more powerful VD-7 engines were installed, together with an increase in fuel capacity, resulting in an increased range of up to 11,850km/7359 miles. Air-refuelling increased range even further up to 15,400km/9563 miles, which made these aircraft the first strategic bombers capable of delivering their payload deep into enemy territory and returning to base. The first flight of this version, designated M-4/3M, took place in March 1956, and service deployment started in 1958.

The M-4/3M/M-6 ("Bison-B" to NATO) had a slightly larger wing than the A, a longer nose fitted with a refuelling probe, greater fuel load, more thrust and an improved bombing/

navigation system. Although this version was primarily a free-fall strategic bomber, it could also serve as a tanker when fitted with removable bomb-bay refuelling kit.

The reliability of the VD-7 engines caused concerns and consequently, between 1958 and 1960, the M-4 was fitted with new RD-3M-500A engines – this version is known as the M-4/3MS.

In 1960, the M-4/3MD bomber version was developed, with a slightly larger wing, a redesigned, sharper nose, shorter and relocated nose refuelling probe, and a larger tail radome. Known to NATO as the "Bison-C", this aircraft was principally a free-fall strategic bomber, but could also serve as a tanker.

In the late 1970s a single 3M bomber was converted for transporting the huge components for the Energiya-Buran space launch system to the Baikonur launch site. Propellant tanks and even the Buran orbiter itself were placed on external mounting points on top of a strengthened fuselage. A new two-fin tail was added to the aircraft for extra stability.

The aircraft carried out a total of 150 flights in the early 1980s. A total of 93 aircraft were built, and the 3M bombers remained in Soviet service until the end of the 1980s, when they were scrapped in accordance with strategic force reductions treaty agreements.

ABOVE RIGHT: **The "Bison C" had a short refuelling probe on the nose, and with its great range, it was suited to the reconnaissance role.**
RIGHT AND BELOW: **These two photographs were taken from US Navy aircraft 16 years apart, and little seems to have changed. The Soviet bomber gets close to US interests and an F-4 goes to escort the Bison away. The picture on the right is a "Bison C", while the aircraft below is a "Bison B", with a longer refuelling probe. The M-4 was one of the earliest Soviet aircraft equipped for IFR.**

## Myasishchev M-4/3M

**First flight:** January 20, 1953
**Power:** Four Soloviev 13,000kg/28,613lb thrust D-15 turbojets
**Armament:** Six defensive 23mm/0.9in cannon; up to 9000kg/19,809lb of various munitions carried in internal bomb bay
**Size:** Wingspan – 50.48m/165ft 7.5in
Length – 47.2m/154ft 10in
Height – 14.1m/46ft
Wing area – 309m²/3326sq ft
**Weights** Empty – 80,000kg/176,080lb
Maximum take-off – 170,000kg/374,170lb
**Performance:** Maximum speed – 900kph/560mph
Ceiling – 15,000m/49,200ft
Range – 11,000km/6835 miles
Climb – Not available

# North American A3J/A-5 Vigilante

In November 1953, North American Aviation began work on a design project for an all-weather long-range carrier-based strike aircraft capable of delivering a nuclear weapon at speeds of up to Mach 2. To meet the needs of the design, the team proposed an aircraft so advanced in many ways that it is fair to say that when the Vigilante appeared, no other aircraft had incorporated so many technological innovations.

The first prototype, the YA3J-1, was rolled out on May 16, 1958, and was officially named Vigilante. The first flight took place on August 31, 1958, and the aircraft went supersonic for the first time on September 5. A second prototype entered the test-flight programme in November that year. The first production A3J-1s soon followed, and the sixth Vigilante constructed made 14 launches and landings on the USS *Saratoga* in July 1960.

The demands made on an aircraft flying at twice the speed of sound are considerable, and special measures have to be taken to ensure that systems continue to function in this very harsh environment. In the case of the Vigilante, pure nitrogen was used instead of hydraulic fluid in some of the airframe's hottest areas. The Vigilante was structurally unusual in that major elements were made of titanium to protect against aerodynamic heating, and the wing skins were machined as one piece from aluminium-lithium alloy – gold plate was used as a heat-reflector in the engine bays.

Advanced aerodynamic features included a small high-loaded swept wing with powerful flaps and a one-piece powered vertical tail. Revolutionary fully variable engine inlets were fitted to slow down supersonic air to subsonic speed

TOP: **The highly advanced Vigilante gave the US Navy a Mach 2 strike capability.** ABOVE: **An RA-5C is readied for launch from the flight deck of the USS *Forrestal* in the Atlantic Ocean.**

before it reached the engine, thus producing maximum performance from the engines at any speed. A fully retractable refuelling probe was built into the forward port fuselage ahead of the pilot's cockpit.

The A3J-1 Vigilante also featured some extremely advanced electronics for the time, including the first production fly-by-wire control system which, although a mechanical system, was retained as back-up. Bombing and navigation computations were carried out by an airborne digital computer and the aircraft had the first operational head-up display (HUD). The aircraft's radar had early terrain-avoidance features, lessening the pilot's workload at low level.

ABOVE: **The RA-5Cs were either all new or converted from the nuclear strike A-5A.** RIGHT: **During the Vietnam War, US Navy RA-5Cs were the "sharp" end of the world's most advanced military reconnaissance system.**

In December 1960, the Vigilante set a new world altitude record for its class when it carried a 1000kg/2403lb payload to a height of 27,893m/91,451ft, exceeding the then record by 6.4km/4 miles.

The Vigilante's nuclear weapon was stored in a unique internal weapons bay without bomb-bay doors in the aircraft belly. Instead of the nuclear bomb being dropped, the weapon (mounted in a long duct that extended back between the two engines) was ejected to the rear during release. This was a complex system, and was prone to technical problems.

The first squadron deployment occurred in August 1962 aboard the USS *Enterprise* on its first cruise, and in September that year the A3J-1 was redesignated A-5A under the new Tri-Service designation system. Shortly thereafter, the US Navy's strategic deterrent mission was assumed by nuclear-powered submarine Polaris missiles, and further procurement of the A-5A was halted after only 59 had been

built. Most were returned to North American for conversion to RA-5C standard – 53 were eventually rebuilt as RA-5Cs and were joined in service by 55 new production aircraft. The RA-5C retained the bomber version's very high-speed performance and was capable of electromagnetic, optical and electronic reconnaissance. The type was used to great effect by the US Seventh fleet during carrier air wing operations in the Vietnam War. The US Navy's last RA-5C fleet squadron was disbanded in September 1979.

RIGHT AND BELOW: **The RA-5C could carry out photographic, electronic and electromagnetic reconnaissance.**

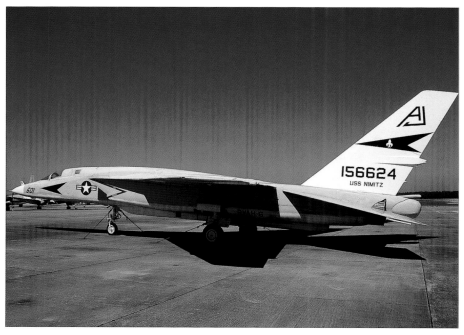

## North American A-5 Vigilante

**First flight:** August 31, 1958 (YA3J-1)
**Power:** Two General Electric 7332kg/16,150lb afterburning thrust J79-2 turbojets
**Armament:** One Mk 27, Mk 28 or Mk 43 nuclear bomb in the linear weapons bay, plus one Mk 43 nuclear or a pair of Mk 83 or Mk 84 conventional bombs on weapons pylon beneath each wing
**Size:** Wingspan – 16.15m/53ft
Length – 23.11m/75ft 10in
Height – 5.92m/19ft 5in
Wing area – 70.05m²/754sq ft
**Weights:** Empty – 17,252kg/38,000lb
Maximum take-off – 36,320kg/80,000lb
**Performance:** Maximum speed – 2230kph/1385mph
Ceiling – 20,435m/67,000ft
Range – 5150km/3200 miles
Climb – 2440m/8000ft per minute

# North American F-100 Super Sabre

The Super Sabre was the world's first supersonic combat aircraft, and was developed by North American from 1949 as a successor to the company's highly successful F-86 Sabre. North American had considered ways to significantly improve the performance of the F-86 Sabre to achieve supersonic speeds in level flight. Design progressed to the Sabre 45, the "45" coming from the angle of the wings' sweepback – the new aircraft was soon designated F-100 Super Sabre.

The aircraft, which made great use of heat-resisting titanium for the first time, was developed very quickly. At Edwards Air Force Base on May 25, 1953, the prototype exceeded the speed of sound on its first flight, giving a taste of the

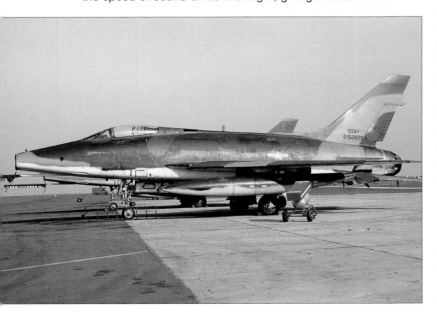

ABOVE AND BELOW LEFT: **The F-100 Super Sabre, the world's first supersonic combat aircraft. Early problems were rectified, and from early 1955 the type became a key USAF type.**

performance to come. On October 29, 1953, with Lieutenant Colonel Pete Everest at the controls, the first production aircraft set a new world speed record of 1215kph/755mph over a 15km/9.3 mile course at an altitude of around 30m/98ft above the ground.

In 1954, the US Air Force's 479th Fighter Wing became the world's first supersonic air combat unit. However, a series of catastrophic inflight failures led to the type being grounded until early 1955. After the wings and fin were reworked to eradicate stability problems, 200 F-100As went on to give sterling service in the USAF. On February 26, 1955, test-pilot George F. Smith ejected from an F-100 at supersonic speed, believed to be the first person to do so.

Eisenhower's administration was keen to build its nuclear forces, and the USAF's Tactical Air Command was tasked with delivering nuclear weapons – hitherto the sole responsibility of Strategic Air Command. The F-100 was the only likely candidate in the inventory, so from early 1954 design work began on the fighter-bomber F-100C.

The improved and more powerful F-100C and later D fighter-bombers reached the Cold War front lines in 1956–7. The C-model had inflight refuelling capability to extend the already impressive range, and a more powerful engine. On August 20, 1955 an F-100C, piloted by Colonel Horace Hanes, set the world's first supersonic speed record of 1323kph/822mph.

The D-model is thought to be the first dedicated fighter-bomber version since the C was a fighter simply modified for the job. The F-100D (first flight on January 24, 1956) was built in greater numbers than any other version and carried ECM equipment as well as a low-altitude bombing system for "tossing" nuclear weapons. It also featured the first autopilot designed for a supersonic jet. A total of 1274 D-models were built in 19 production blocks.

From 1964 to 1971 in the Vietnam War, USAF F-100s saw extensive service in the fighter, reconnaissance and ground-attack roles, flying more missions than the manufacturer's P-51 Mustang had in World War II. The first F-100 Vietnam mission took place on June 9, 1964. Operating from Da Nang in South Vietnam, they were ordered to bomb a target in the Plaines des Jarres in Laos. Super Sabre operations were mainly conducted from four modern bases built for USAF aircraft – Bien Hoa, Phan Rang, Phu Cat and Tuy Hoa. Although the F-100 was not well suited to the extreme structural loads produced during low-level high-speed bombing, the F-100D alone flew 360,283 sorties between 1964 and 1971. During this time, only 186 aircraft were lost to anti-aircraft fire, and none in air combat. Due to the comparatively short range of the aircraft, it was primarily operated over South Vietnam.

Super Sabres retired from USAF service in 1972, but remained in use with Air National Guard units until 1980. F-100s were supplied to Denmark, France, Taiwan and Turkey, Turkey finally retiring the type in the mid-1980s.

Two-seat and reconnaissance versions were also produced, and by the time production stopped in 1959, almost 2300 Super Sabres had been built.

TOP: **The F-100C fighter-bomber enabled the USA to increase its nuclear forces very rapidly.** ABOVE: **This F-100 wears a typical gaudy pre-Vietnam USAF livery.**
BELOW: **Denmark operated single-seat F-100Ds and F-100F two-seat trainers.**

### North American F-100D Super Sabre

**First flight:** May 25, 1953 (prototype)
**Power:** Pratt & Whitney 7718kg/17,000lb afterburning thrust J57-P21 turbojet
**Armament:** Four 20mm/0.78in cannon; six underwing load points for up to 3405kg/7500lb of weapons
**Size:** Wingspan – 11.81m/38ft 9in
Length – 15.09m/49ft 6in
Height – 4.95m/16ft 3in
Wing area – 35.77m²/385sq ft
**Weights:** Empty – 9534kg/21,000lb
Maximum take-off – 15,813kg/34,832lb
**Performance:** Maximum speed – 1390kph/864mph
Ceiling – 13,725m/45,000ft
Range – 3210km/1995 miles with external drop tanks
Climb – 4877m/16,000ft per minute

# Northrop Grumman B-2 Spirit

When the Northrop B-2 Spirit was rolled out of its hangar and first shown to the world on November 22, 1988, expressions such as "futuristic" and "otherworldly" were used to describe it. These were coincidentally the same terms used to describe Northrop's revolutionary YB-49 flying-wing bomber of 1947.

The B-2 Spirit "stealth" aircraft is a strategic long-range heavy bomber whose all-altitude, low-observable stealth technology gives it the capability to penetrate the world's most sophisticated air defences. Conceived during the Cold War, the B-2 was designed to slip through enemy radar defences without being detected and then drop up to 16 nuclear bombs on key targets. Its first flight was July 17, 1989.

The B-2's low observability is derived from a combination of reduced infrared, acoustic, electromagnetic, visual and radar signatures. These signatures make it difficult for even the most sophisticated defensive systems to detect, track and engage the B-2. While many aspects of the aircraft's low observability remain classified, the B-2's composite graphite-epoxy materials, special coatings (such as radar-absorbent paint on its leading edge) and flying-wing design are all known to contribute to its "stealthiness".

The B-2's low-observability means that it does not need a fleet of support aircraft (jammers, anti-radar aircraft or fighter escort aircraft) to accomplish a mission, and its large payload allows it to do the work of many smaller attack aircraft. The revolutionary blending of low-observability technologies with

TOP: **The number of claimed UFO sightings generated by the B-2, especially during its top-secret development years, are probably high. Even knowing what this flying object is, it still appears other-worldly.** ABOVE: **A rare view of the B-2 with its bomb-bay doors open.**

high aerodynamic efficiency and large payload gives the B-2 important advantages over existing bombers. Its low observability gives it greater freedom of action at high altitudes, thus increasing its range and providing a better field of view for the aircraft's top-secret sensors. The US Air Force has published a representative mission scenario showing that two B-2s armed with precision weapons can do the job that 75 conventional aircraft would normally be required to carry out.

### Northrop Grumman B-2 Spirit

**First flight:** July 17, 1989
**Power:** Four General Electric 7854kg/17,300lb thrust F-118-GE-100 engines
**Armament:** 18,160kg/40,000lb of weapons, including free-fall or retarded conventional or nuclear (strategic or tactical) weapons carried in two rotary launcher assemblies
**Size:** Wingspan – 52.12m/172ft
Length – 20.9m/69ft
Height – 5.1m/17ft
Wing area – Approximately 464.5m²/5000sq ft
**Weights:** Empty – 69,780kg/153,700lb
Maximum take-off – 170,704kg/376,000lb
**Performance:** Maximum speed – 915ph/568mph
Ceiling – 15,250m/50,000ft
Range – 9654km/6000 miles
Climb – Not available

ABOVE: **Radar-absorbent paint on the aircraft's leading edge adds to the B-2's "invisibility" to radar.** RIGHT: **During the development of the B-2, some of the testing team of the 1947 YB-49 were consulted about the handling characteristics of the 1940s flying wing.**

The B-2 has a crew of two, a pilot in the left seat and mission commander in the right, so only four crew members are put at risk in this mission, compared to 132 in the conventional.

Capable of delivering both conventional and nuclear munitions, the B-2 brings massive firepower to bear in a short time anywhere on the globe through previously impenetrable defences, and threatens its most valued and heavily defended targets. The unrefuelled range of the B-2 is approximately 9654km/6000 miles.

The B-2 made its combat debut on March 24, 1999, as part of Operation Allied Force when two aircraft dropped 32,908kg/2000lb joint direct-attack munitions (JDAMs) on Serbian targets during a marathon 31-hour, non-stop mission from Whiteman Air Force Base in Missouri, USA. The combination of its all-weather precision capability and the aircraft's ability to penetrate lethal defences put the enemy's high-value fixed targets at risk. Over the course of Operation Allied Force, 45 B-2 sorties by a total of six aircraft delivered 656 JDAMs on critical targets in the then Federal Republic of Yugoslavia. The B-2 was responsible for destroying 33 per cent of all Serbian targets in the first eight weeks.

During Operation Enduring Freedom in Afghanistan, the B-2 flew a total of six missions on the first three days of the war. Each sortie took 70 hours, including the flight to Afghanistan, a turn-around at Diego Garcia for a new crew and the flight back to Whiteman AFB, home of the B-2.

This remarkable aircraft, each costing around 1.2 billion US dollars, gives the USA the edge over potential enemies whose targets, if detectable, can without doubt be attacked by the 21 B-2s of the US Air Force.

# Panavia Tornado IDS

Originally known as the Multi-Role Combat Aircraft (MRCA), the Tornado came about as a joint venture between the UK, Italy and Germany, with each nation assuming responsibility for the manufacture of specific aircraft sections. A new tri-national company, Panavia, was set up in Germany to build the Tornado, and the resulting aircraft was a technological, political and administrative triumph, given the problems that had to be overcome. Each nation assembled its own air force's aircraft, and power for all was provided by Rolls-Royce-designed Turbo-Union engines.

The first aircraft took to the air on August 14, 1974 at Manching, Germany. The initial RAF requirement was for 220 Tornado GR1 strike aircraft, and the first of these entered service with the Tri-national Tornado Training Establishment (TTTE) at RAF Cottesmore in 1980. The first front-line squadron to re-equip with the Tornado was IX Squadron at Honington from June 1982. Nuclear-capable Tornado GR1s eventually equipped a total of ten front-line squadrons deployed in Britain and Germany ready for war with the Warsaw Pact.

The Tornado is one of the world's few variable-geometry aircraft whose "swing wings" enable optimum performance at any speed. Swept forward to 25 degrees, wing slats and flaps can be extended providing high lift for take-off and landing. Once the aircraft becomes airborne, the wings are swept back to 45 degrees for normal flying or 67 degrees for high-speed operations.

TOP: **Tornado GR1 – the pod at the tip of the port wing is a Sky Shadow ECM pod, while beneath the tip of the starboard wing sits a chaff and flare dispenser.** ABOVE: **The RAF's first swing-wing combat aircraft, the Panavia Tornado.**

GR1s were upgraded to GR4 standard by adding forward-looking infrared (FLIR), a wide-angle head-up display (HUD), improved cockpit displays, night-vision goggle (NVG) compatibility, new avionics and weapons systems, updated computer software and global positioning system (GPS). The upgrade also allowed for carriage of the Storm Shadow stand-off missile, Brimstone advanced anti-armour weapon, advanced reconnaissance pods and the thermal imaging airborne laser designator (TIALD) targeting pod. A separate programme covered an integrated Defensive Aids Suite, consisting of the radar warning receiver, Sky Shadow radar jamming pod and BOZ-107 chaff and flare dispenser. These upgrades enable the Tornado to operate in the harshest air defence environments.

ABOVE: **RAF Tornados were in the thick of the Gulf War air campaign in 1991, with six lost to SAM missiles.** ABOVE RIGHT: **The radar-transparent nose cone houses the Tornado's ground-mapping and terrain-following radar.** RIGHT: **With wings in the fully-swept position, the Tornado bomber can reach speeds of up to 2336kph/1452mph.**

The heart of the Tornado GR4's navigation and attack system is the main computer, which takes its primary reference from an inertial navigation system (INS) supplemented by global positioning system (GPS). Targeting information can come from the FLIR, TIALD, laser ranger and marked target seeker (LRMTS) or visually. Among the Tornado's available weaponry are Paveway laser- or GPS-guided bombs, ballistic or retarded "dumb" 454kg/1000lb bombs, Cluster Bomb Units (CBU), Storm Shadow, Brimstone, Air-Launched Anti-Radiation (ALARM) and Sidewinder missiles, and a single 27mm/1.05in cannon. A dedicated reconnaissance version, the GR4A, is also in RAF service.

The Tornado GR4 is optimized for low-level penetration of enemy airspace for precision attacks against high-value targets. The GR4 has fly-by-wire flight controls with mechanical back-up, and can operate in all weather conditions, using terrain-following radar (TFR) and ground-mapping radar (GMR) to guide the aircraft and identify the target.

In 1991, RAF Tornados played a vital strike role in the Gulf War, carrying out more than 1500 bombing raids over Iraq. Six Tornados were lost, half in low-level strikes, and all were downed by surface-to-air missiles.

A year later, Tornados of 617 Squadron, the famous Dambusters, participated in Operation Fural, patrolling no-fly zones in southern Iraq.

In January 2003, Royal Air Force Tornados were assigned to Operation Telic, the Coalition liberation of Iraq. This operation marked a number of firsts for the GR4: No.617 Squadron debuted the Storm Shadow stand-off missile, and Enhanced Paveway II and III GPS-guided bombs were used, as were improved ALARM II anti-radar missiles. The Tornado is expected to remain the backbone of Britain's air-strike capability for many years to come.

---

### Panavia Tornado GR4

**First flight:** October 27, 1979

**Power:** Two Turbo-Union 7298kg/16,075lb afterburning thrust RB199-103 turbofans

**Armament:** One Mauser 27mm/1.05in cannon, plus Sidewinder missiles carried for self-defence; up to 8172kg/18,000lb of ordnance, including Paveway 2 or 3 laser-guided bombs, ballistic or retarded "dumb" 454kg/1000lb bombs, Cluster Bombs, Storm Shadow, Brimstone, Air-Launched Anti-Radiation Missile (ALARM)

**Size:** Wingspan – 13.91m/45ft 8in, spread 8.60m/28ft 3in, swept
Length – 16.70m/54ft 10in
Height – 5.95m/19ft 6in
Wing area – 26.6m²/286.3sq ft at 25 degrees sweepback

**Weights:** Empty – 13,901kg/30,620lb
Maximum takeoff – 27,975kg/61,620lb

**Performance:** Maximum speed – 2336kph/1452mph
Ceiling – 15,250m/50,000ft
Range – 2778km/1726 miles
Climb – 9150m/30,000ft in 2 minutes

# Republic F-105 Thunderchief

The Republic F-105 Thunderchief – the "Thud" – was the first purpose-designed supersonic tactical fighter-bomber to be developed, and it is widely considered to be one of the greatest-ever single-engine jet-powered combat aircraft. It was also the biggest single-seat, single-engine combat aircraft in history, boasting a large internal bomb bay and unique forward-swept engine inlets in the wing roots. This potent and versatile aircraft could also fly at speeds in excess of Mach 2. The F-105 was the only jet fighter to refuel from a side-fuselage boom, and was the first jet fighter to be armed with a Vulcan 20mm/0.78in cannon.

The F-105 developed from a project begun in 1951 by Republic Aviation to find a supersonic tactical fighter-bomber to replace the F-84. The primary mission for the large F-105 was to be capable of a nuclear strike. The prototype first flew in October 1955, but the first production version, the F-105B of which 75 were built, did not enter US Air Force service until May 1958. On December 11, 1959, an F-105B flown by

Brigadier General Joseph Moore set a new world speed record of 1957.32kph/1216.48mph over a 100km/62-mile closed circuit. Perhaps the greatest tribute to the Thud is that in May 1963, the F-105B was chosen to replace the F-100C Super Sabres as the standard aircraft of the crack USAF Thunderbirds Flight Demonstration Team.

The first flight of the F-105D all-weather strike fighter, the first Thunderchief version to possess true all-weather capability, was made on June 9, 1959, and deliveries to the USAF followed within a year. The F-105D looked similar to the earlier B-model, but had a larger nose radome containing a radar that enabled the aircraft to carry out visual or blind attacks with missiles or bombs. The US Air Force in Europe first received the F-105D in May 1961, and the type equipped two tactical fighter wings based in Germany.

No C or E-models were produced; the F-105F was a two-seat, dual-purpose trainer-fighter, while the G-series were modified F-models equipped with a comprehensive electronic

RIGHT: **The "Thud" was the largest single-seat combat aircraft in history.** BELOW: **The F-105F was a two-seat trainer, but with combat facility.**

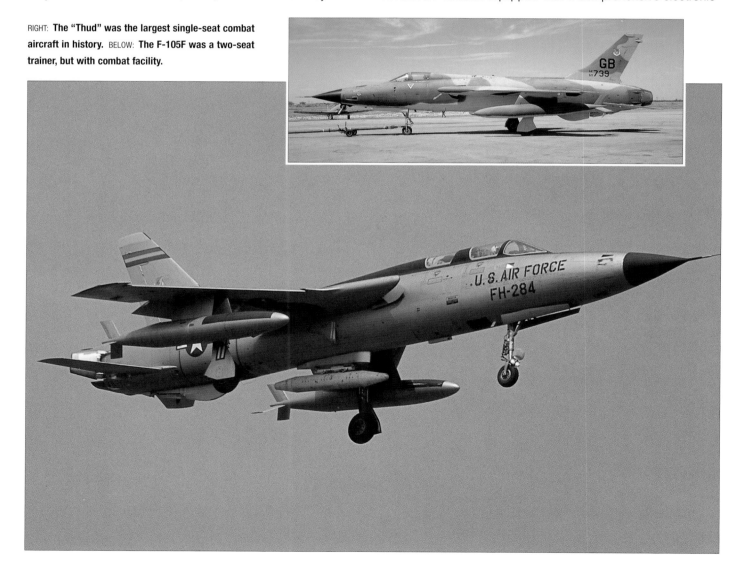

countermeasures suite. F-105Gs were nicknamed "Wild Weasels" and were tasked with clearing the way for heavy bombers by jamming enemy radar and eliminating surface-to-air missile sites.

The F-105 was the backbone of USAF tactical air power in the Vietnam War and the D-model carried out more air strikes against North Vietnam than any other aircraft in the US aircraft inventory. From 1965 to 1968, three-quarters of all US air strikes against Vietnam were carried out by F-105s. By the end of the war, the versatile F-105 was credited with 25 MiG kills, but was also found to have suffered more losses than any other US type. Over half of all the D-models built (610) were destroyed in the war, and F-105 pilots were thought to have only a 75 per cent chance of surviving 100 missions over North Vietnam.

Production of the F-105 ended in 1964 after a total of 833 aircraft had been built, but unlike many US fighters, the type was never exported to foreign countries. The F-105 continued in USAF service until as late as 1980, but some continued to serve in the Air Force Reserve and the Air National Guard until 1984.

## Republic F-105D Thunderchief

**First Flight:** October 22, 1955 (YF-105A)
**Power:** One Pratt & Whitney 10,896kg/24,000lb afterburning thrust J75-P-19W turbojet
**Armament:** One 20mm/0.78in cannon; 6356kg/14,000lb of mixed ordnance carried internally and externally
**Size:** Wingspan – 10.59m/34ft 9in
Length – 19.61m/64ft 4in
Height – 5.97m/19ft 7in
Wing area – 35.77m²/385sq ft
**Weights:** Empty – 12,485kg/27,500lb
Maximum take-off – 23,988kg/52,838lb
**Performance:** Maximum speed – 2237kph/1390mph
Ceiling – 12,566m/41,200ft
Range – 3846km/2390 miles
Climb – 10,492m/34,400ft per minute

ABOVE LEFT: **The F-105D carried out more bombing missions than any other US type.**
ABOVE: **The F-105G "Wild Weasel" was a dedicated anti-radar aircraft which could jam and destroy enemy radar.**
LEFT: **Over half of all F-105s built fell to North Vietnam defences during the war.**

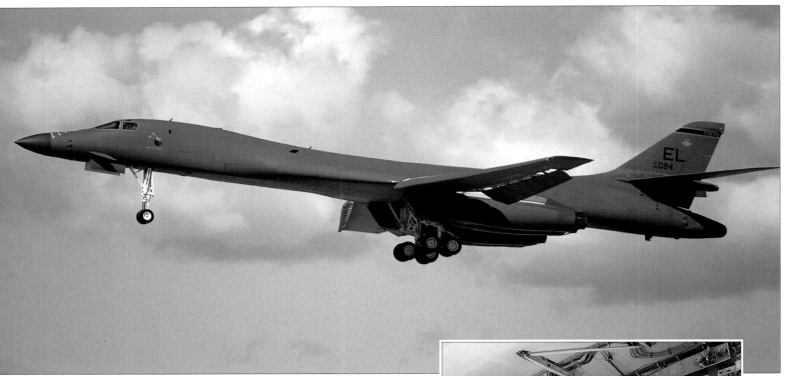

# Rockwell B-1 Lancer

The B-1 was designed as a nuclear weapons delivery system in response to a 1965 USAF requirement for a high-speed, low-level replacement for the B-52. Construction of the first prototype B-1A began in late 1972, and the prototype flew on December 23, 1974. By the end of June 1977, three prototypes had made 118 flights with 646 hours of flying time. Spiralling costs led to the project's cancellation in 1977 but interestingly, flight tests of the four B-1As continued until 1981.

High-level military and political lobbying led to the B-1's resurrection by the Reagan administration in 1982. The improved production version which first flew on October 18, 1984 was the B-1B. This differed from the B-1A by having updated avionics, strengthened undercarriage, ejection seats instead of the original crew-escape pod, and the ability to carry weapons externally. The first B-1B was delivered to Dyess Air Force Base, Texas, in June 1985, and operational capability was achieved on October 1, 1986. The last of 100 B-1Bs was delivered on May 2, 1988, each with a unit cost of 200 million US dollars.

The Rockwell B-1B was one of the last long-range strategic bombers to be built, and is capable of penetrating very sophisticated defences. The aircraft is the backbone of America's long-range bomber force, providing massive and rapid delivery of precision and non-precision weapons against any potential adversary anywhere around the globe on short notice. The B-1 uses shorter runways and flies lower and faster than the B-52, can carry more than twice the bomb load, and has a smaller radar profile than the Boeing bomber, making radar detection harder for the enemy.

TOP: **The B1-B, among the last of the true long-range strategic bombers.** ABOVE: **Inside the capacious bomb bay of the Lancer, which can carry up to 34,050kg/75,000lb.**

The ongoing Conventional Mission Upgrade Program is significantly enhancing the B-1B's capability. This increases the aircraft's accuracy and survivability by integrating "smart" and stand-off weapons and onboard countermeasures. The B-1B AN/ALQ 161A defensive avionics system detects and counters enemy radar threats, including missiles attacking from the rear. It defends the aircraft by applying the appropriate countermeasures, such as electronic jamming or dispensing chaff and flares.

The B-1B's radar and inertial navigation equipment enable its crew to navigate globally, update mission profiles and target co-ordinates inflight, and precision-bomb without the need for ground-based navigation aids. Numerous upgrades and modifications have been carried out or are under consideration to keep the Lancer at the technological forefront.

B-1s were used extensively in the 2003 war in Iraq. Operating from Guam, B-1s would head for Iraq, and when nearing Iraqi airspace, drop down to low level while maintaining a high speed. After striking a target or targets, the aircraft would then rendezvous with a tanker for mid-air refuelling. On April 7, 2003 a B-1 was doing just that when an airborne control aircraft made contact, telling the crew, "this is the big one", and directed them to a new high-priority target which had to be struck within ten minutes. Intelligence sources had learned that a high-level Iraqi leadership meeting was underway in a suburb of Baghdad. Prompt action was required to possibly remove the leadership of the enemy regime, and the B-1 was the weapon for the task. The aircraft found the location and dropped four precision-guided 908kg/2000lb bombs on the target – within ten minutes.

Within that time, the crew had planned an escape route, assessed enemy air defences, maintained contact with airborne and ground controllers, selected appropriate weapons and dialled-in the target's co-ordinates. Due to the suburban location, prevention of civilian casualties and collateral damage was a primary concern. To reduce the danger to innocent people and nearby property, mission planners chose the precise Version 3 of the GBU-31 joint direct attack munition (JDAM). The bomb is a hard-target penetrating bomb that buries itself before exploding, thus minimizing fragmentation into surrounding locations. The B-1's global-positioning system guided JDAMs to strike within 12m/40ft of the target. During the 2003 campaign over Iraq, B-1s used around 2100 JDAMs against airfields, bunkers and leadership targets, with a claimed successful targeting of 99 per cent.

TOP: **With wings in the fully swept position, the B-1 can maintain speeds in excess of Mach 1.** ABOVE: **Dropping parachute-retarded bombs.**
BELOW: **A B-1B of the 28th Bomb Wing, Ellsworth AFB.**

## Rockwell B-1B Lancer

**First Flight:** October 18, 1984

**Power:** Four General Electric 13,974kg/30,780lb afterburning thrust F-101-GE-102 turbofans

**Armament:** Maximum internal bomb load of 34,050kg/75,000lb of conventional or nuclear weapons, cruise missiles or smart weaponry

**Size:** Wingspan – 41.8m/137ft, unswept
24.1m/79ft, swept
Length – 44.5m/146ft
Height – 10.4m/34ft
Wing area – 181m²/1950sq ft

**Weights:** Empty – 87,168kg/192,000lb
Maximum take-off – 216,558kg/477,000lb

**Performance:** Maximum speed – 1448kph/900mph plus
Ceiling – 9150m/30,000ft plus
Combat radius – 9654km/6000 miles
Climb – Not available

# Sepecat Jaguar

This potent fighter-bomber was originally designed to meet a joint 1965 Anglo-French requirement for a dual-role advanced/operational trainer and tactical support aircraft. The aircraft was to be built and operated by both countries. The Royal Air Force initially intended to use the aircraft purely as an advanced trainer to replace its Hawker Hunter and Folland Gnat trainers, but this was later changed to the offensive support role on cost grounds.

The finished aircraft was capable of flight in excess of the speed of sound, and could be armed with a tactical nuclear weapon. Often dismissed as obsolete, the Jaguar is still able to deliver a heavy payload over great distances and with considerable accuracy in most weathers.

The Jaguar, coincidentally developed in parallel with Concorde, another Anglo-French project, was the first example of an aircraft developed by Britain with a partner nation for use by the RAF and another air force. Britain built Jaguar wings, tails and the rear fuselage, while France produced the centre and forward fuselage sections.

The French prototype flew on September 8, 1968, while the first Jaguar to be built in Britain, XW560, had its maiden flight at Warton in October 1969. With Wing Commander Jimmy Dell at the controls, the aircraft went supersonic on its first flight.

The British and French air forces each placed orders for 200 aircraft, the RAF opting for 165 single-seat and 35 two-seat aircraft. Deliveries to the RAF began in 1973 and more

TOP AND ABOVE: **When the RAF first considered what became the Jaguar, they were only looking for an advanced trainer. Four decades later, the "Jag" is serving the RAF as a counter-air, close-support and tactical-reconnaissance aircraft.**

than three decades on, the Jaguar continues to equip RAF as well as Armée de l'Air units.

The Jaguar has a robust landing gear designed for use from rough forward airstrips for war in Europe – Royal Air Force Jaguars with full bomb loads were test-operated from lengths of European motorway, which might have been used instead of airfields had the Cold War heated up. The Jaguar force of RAF Germany held the line in West Germany until the Tornado GR1 entered service.

In the early 2000s, the RAF's Jaguar fleet underwent a major upgrade programme and was designated the Jaguar GR3 (T4 for the two-seat variant). The upgrade included improved avionics, including global positioning system (GPS), night-vision goggles (NVG) helmet-mounted sight and new head-up display (HUD) and head-down displays (HDD).

RIGHT: **RAF Jaguars are all based at RAF Coltishall.**
MIDDLE RIGHT: **During the Cold War, the RAF's Jaguars frequently trained in Arctic conditions, but the type's engines are now being upgraded for high and hot operations.**
BELOW RIGHT: **The wingspan of the Jaguar is considerably less than that of the famous Spitfire.** BELOW: **The RAF Jaguar fleet, recently upgraded to GR3 standard, can carry retard and freefall bombs, as well as the Paveway II and III laser-guided bombs.**

The Jaguar is capable of carrying 454kg/1000lb retard and freefall bombs, cluster munitions, laser-guided bombs, rocket and two 30mm/1.18in Aden cannon. For self-defence, two AIM-9L Sidewinder air-to-air missiles can be mounted on the over-wing hardpoints, and may be launched via the helmet-mounted sight system. These are complemented by a rear warning radar, an electronic countermeasures (ECM) pod to jam enemy radar, as well as chaff and flare dispensers to confuse radar and heat-seeking missiles respectively.

The aircraft can carry an external fuel tank on the centreline pylon, or two tanks beneath the wings. In the reconnaissance role, the externally mounted Jaguar Reconnaissance Pod can provide horizon-to-horizon coverage from medium and low level.

RAF and French Jaguars participated extensively in the 1991 Gulf War, and British aircraft have been subsequently involved in many operations in the Middle East and the Balkans. The type regularly deploys for exercises to North America, Europe and the Middle East, operating in diverse conditions from the desert to the Arctic Circle. On February 6, 2003, RAF Jaguars were deployed to the Gulf for action against Iraq again, and carried out many missions as part of the liberation of Iraq.

In August 1976, an export version named Jaguar International first flew. The type was ultimately exported to Ecuador, Oman, Nigeria and India.

## Sepecat Jaguar

**First Flight:** September 8, 1968
**Power:** Two Rolls-Royce Turboméca 3650kg/ 8040lb afterburning thrust Adour 104 turbofans
**Armament:** Two 30mm/1.18in cannon; 4540kg/ 10,000lb of mixed ordnance carried externally, plus overwing pylons for air-to-air missiles
**Size:** Wingspan – 8.69m/28ft 6in
Length – 16.83m/55ft 2.5in
Height – 4.89m/16ft 0.5in
Wing area – 24.18m²/260.28sq ft
**Weights:** Empty – 7000kg/15,407lb
Maximum take-off – 15,700kg/34,555lb
**Performance:** Maximum speed – 1699kph/ 1056mph
Ceiling – 13,725m/45,000ft plus
Combat radius – 1408km/875 miles
Climb – Not available

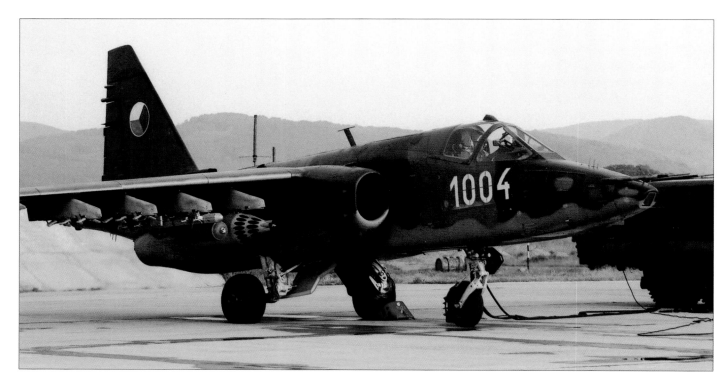

# Sukhoi Su-25

The single-seat Su-25 first flew in 1975, and became a hard-hitting ground-attack aircraft first tested in battle during the Soviet invasion of Afghanistan. The aircraft was designed for combat against NATO forces, and is the only dedicated close-support aircraft in the Russian inventory. Its job was to help control the main battle area by launching devastating precision attacks on mobile or stationary enemy ground forces while loitering over the high-risk battle area. The Su-25 can also engage low-speed air targets.

The aircraft was designed for the same purpose as the US A-10 and, like its American counterpart, is a very rugged aircraft. However, the Su-25 is smaller than the A-10, and can fly around 273kph/170mph faster than the American aircraft. Although many aircraft are claimed to be suitable for forward-location rough-field operations, the Su-25 really is. All servicing equipment, including a fuel pump, can be stored in a container carried beneath the aircraft's wing. The aircraft's engines have the remarkable capability to run, at least for short flights, on most fuels to be found in a combat environment, including aviation fuel, petrol and diesel.

Like the A-10, the Su-25 is armed with a devastating 30mm/1.18in cannon for attacking armour. The twin-barrel gun is installed in the port underside of the fuselage and can fire its 250 rounds at a rate of 3000 rounds per minute. SPPU-22 gun pods can be carried on the underwing pylons, each housing GSh-23 23mm/0.9in twin-barrel guns with 260 rounds of ammunition.

The aircraft's ten pylons can carry up to 4400kg/9684lb of ordnance, from self-defence air-to-air missiles to anti-shipping missiles, anti-tank munitions and cluster bombs. Air-to-ground

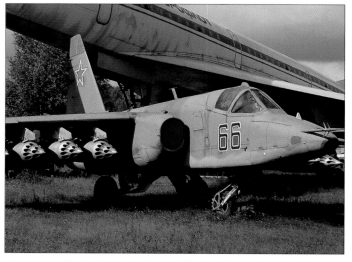

TOP AND ABOVE: **The Su-25, born in the Cold War, is still in use, largely with air forces in the former Eastern bloc. Even so, some have been relegated to museum pieces (above).**

missiles carried include Kh-23 (NATO codename AS-7 Kerry), Kh-25 (AS-10 Karen) and Kh-29 (AS-14 Kedge). The air-to-air missiles carried on the smaller outboard pylons are the R-3S (AA-2D Atoll) and the R-60 (AA-8 Aphid). The aircraft can be fitted with S-24 240mm/9.3in or S-25 330mm/13in guided rockets, UB-32A pods for 57mm/2.22in S-5 rockets and B-8M1 pods for 80mm/3.12in S-8 rockets.

Aircraft and pilot survivability were central to the design. The pilot, like that of the A-10, sits within a thick titanium "bathtub" for protection against ground fire and shrapnel. While many combat aircraft have cable-activated control surfaces, the Su-25 use heavy-duty pushrods that are much less likely to be severed by a stray bullet. The Su-25 carries a total of 256 decoy flares, which it fires 32 at a time when carrying out an attack run to confuse heat-seeking missiles launched from the ground or the air.

Early examples of the Su-25 were rushed to Afghanistan in 1980 for combat evaluation, and a number of modifications to production aircraft were introduced as a result. The engines were originally close together, and attacks by missiles or anti-aircraft fire led to both catching fire even if only one was damaged. Subsequently, engines were well separated and housed in protective stainless steel bays to safeguard against nearby explosions. Following Afghan Stinger missile attacks that ruptured fuel tanks, the tanks on later aircraft were foam-filled to prevent explosions, as well as being armoured on the underside.

Although the Su-25 was known to the West by its NATO codename "Frogfoot", Soviet pilots called the aircraft "Gratch" (rook) due to that bird's ability to get at hard-to-find targets.

Variants of the Su-25 are operated by the Russian Air Force, Russian Naval Aviation forces, Afghanistan, Angola, Belarus, Bulgaria, the Czech Republic, Georgia, Kazakhstan, North Korea, Peru, the Slovak Republic and the Ukraine. The export variant of the aircraft is known as the Su-25K, and an upgraded Su-25K, known as the "Scorpion", has been developed jointly by Tbilisi Aerospace Manufacturing (TAM) of Georgia with Elbit of Israel. The Su-25UTG is the two-seater aircraft-carrier variant fitted with an arrester hook deployed on the 50,800 tonne/50,000-ton Russian Navy aircraft carrier *Admiral Kuznetsov*.

LEFT: **An Su-25 with underwing stores. This aircraft is based at Pardubice in Czechoslovakia with the 30th Attack Regiment, 1992.** BELOW: **One of the most amazing features of the Su-25 is its ability to run on petrol, diesel or aviation fuel.** BOTTOM LEFT: **The Su-25's ten pylons can carry a devastating array of weaponry.**

### Sukhoi Su-25

**First flight:** February 22, 1975

**Power:** Two Tumanski 4500kg/9904lb thrust R-195 turbojets

**Armament:** One 30mm/1.18in cannon; up to 4400kg/9684lb of air-to-air, air-to-surface, anti-tank, anti-radiation missiles, plus guided and cluster bombs, rockets, rocket pods, gun packs, ECM pods and drop tanks

**Size:** Wingspan – 14.36m/47ft 1.5in
Length – 15.53m/50ft 11.5in
Height – 4.8m/15ft 9in
Wing area – 33.7m²/362.75sq ft

**Weights:** Empty – 9500kg/20,909lb
Maximum take-off – 17,600kg/38,738lb

**Performance:** Maximum speed – 975kph/606mph
Ceiling – 7000m/22,965ft
Range – 1249km/776 miles
Climb – 3482m/11,415ft per minute

# Tupolev Tu-22/Tu-22M

The Tu-22 had its beginnings in a 1955 study to produce a supersonic bomber capable of penetrating the most modern air defences at high altitude and high speed to deliver nuclear weapons. The aircraft flew for the first time in September 1959 and went on to become Russia's first successful supersonic bomber. Typically of the time, the aircraft was unknown to the West until its first public appearance in 1961 when ten examples, one of them carrying a cruise missile, took part in a fly-past. This no doubt sent NATO analysts into a frenzy, and they soon codenamed the aircraft "Blinder".

The three-man Tu-22 (pilot, navigator and radio operator/gunner) is most easily recognized by the unusual position of its engines at the base of its fin. The tail also housed a radar-controlled 23mm/0.9in cannon for defence.

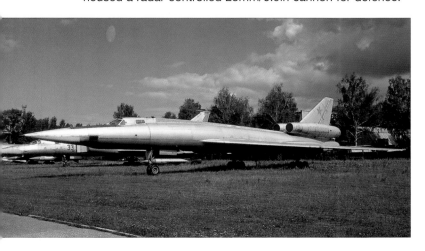

ABOVE: **Since first taking to the air in 1964, the Tu-22M has become a key bomber in the Russian inventory.** BELOW LEFT: **The original Tu-22, from which the Tu-22M was derived, has its engines located at the base of its fin. The Tu-22 was not a swing-wing aircraft like the Tu-22M.**

About 300 Tu-22s were built between 1960 and 1969, the first version being the Tu-22 "Blinder-A" bomber/reconnaissance version carrying free-fall nuclear bombs. The Tu-22K "Blinder-B" was a missile-carrying version armed with AS-4 missiles and a large guidance radar mounted under its nose. The Tu-22R "Blinder-C" was a daylight reconnaissance version with six "windows" in the bomb bay for three pairs of long-range cameras. The Tu-22U "Blinder-D" was a trainer version with the instructor pilot seated in a separate raised cockpit, and the Tu-22P "Blinder-E" was an ECM (electronic countermeasures) version based on Tu-22R. Once the Tu-22s were past their best as bombers, most surviving examples were converted into jamming platforms.

Apart from Russia, who used the Tu-22 into the late 1980s, the type was also operated by Ukraine, Libya and Iraq. The Tu-22 saw action in a number of conflicts, including the Soviet invasion of Afghanistan and the Iran-Iraq War. Iraq used their aircraft against Kurdish rebels in the 1980s, while Libya used their Tu-22s against Chad and Sudan.

Once in service, the Tu-22 offered no great advantage over the Tu-16 that it was intended to replace. The Tu-22 was not built in great numbers, reportedly because of problems with reliability, and Tupolev sought to revise the aircraft's design to produce a much better performance. It was this study

LEFT: **Derived from the Tu-22, the Tu-22M is an all-new aircraft.**
BELOW: **The "swing-wing" Tu-22M can achieve speeds in excess of 1930kph/1200mph.** BOTTOM: **The Tu-22M-3 is the most versatile model, and can carry out a range of very different missions.**

which resulted in the Tu-22M ("Backfire" in NATO-speak), originally a swing-wing version of the Tu-22 which became an all-new aircraft.

The engines on the Tu-22M were changed to the much more powerful Kuznetsov units and were repositioned to the more conventional location in the rear fuselage. The Tu-22M prototype, much altered from the original Tu-22 design, first flew on August 30, 1964. It was another five years before NATO became aware of the new aircraft and was able to codename it "Backfire-A". The first production version (of a total run of around 500 aircraft) was the Tu-22M-2 "Backfire-B", but then in 1980 production switched to the Tu-22M-3 "Backfire-C", fitted with more powerful engines and having revised air intakes. Most importantly, this version can carry a number of Kh-15 (NATO "Kickback") missiles which can be

configured for anti-radar, anti-shipping, conventional or nuclear missions. Around 300 examples of the M-2 have been built, and they are still very much in front-line service with both Russia and the only other operator, Ukraine. A small number of the ECM version, the Tu-22MR, were also built.

## Tupolev Tu-22M-3

**First flight:** August 30, 1964
**Power:** Two KKBM Kuznetsov 25,051kg/55,137lb thrust NK-2512MV turbofans
**Armament:** One 23mm/0.9in cannon in tail; 24,000kg/52,824lb of conventional munitions in bomb bay or three Kh-22 missiles or ten Kh-15 missiles
**Size:** Wingspan – 34.28m/112ft 6in, spread 23.3m/76ft 6in, swept
Length – 42.46m/139ft 4in
Height – 11.05m/36ft
Wing area – 175.8m²/1892.4sq ft
**Weights** Empty – 54,000kg/118,854lb
Maximum take-off – 124,000kg/272,924lb
**Performance:** Maximum speed – 2000kph/ 1242mph
Ceiling – 13,226m/43,394ft
Combat radius – 4000km/2485 miles
Climb – Not available

# Tupolev Tu-95

The Tu-95 (NATO codename "Bear") was probably the most successful post-war Soviet bomber design. In an age of jet-powered bombers, the turboprop-powered Tu-95 had a remarkable range capability and flew at speeds not far behind those of its "enemy" counterparts.

The Tu-95 had an interesting ancestry because its fuselage profile was that of the earlier Tu-4 bomber, which was an unofficial copy of the American B-29 Superfortress. For many, the Bear is an icon of Cold War tension since it was frequently photographed probing UK airspace, escorted by an RAF fighter.

Development of the Tu-95 began in the early 1950s as the Soviet Union looked to increase the reach and destructive capability of their bomber fleet. KB Tupolev proposed an aircraft with four turbo-prop engines that would provide a range of more than 13,000km/8073 miles and speeds of more than 800kph/497mph at altitudes of 10,000m/32,810ft.

The aircraft's 35-degree swept wings (unique in a propeller-driven aircraft) were made with the experience of developing the swept wing for the Tu-16 jet bomber.

As with many aircraft, the success of the design hinged totally on an effective powerplant. The design of the Tu-95 called for turboprops with a power output of around 10,000hp, while the most powerful Russian turboprop available at the time only generated 4800hp. Engine designers Kuznetsov had the job of getting the prototype Bear in the air, and their stop-gap solution while the awesome NK-12 was developed was to use eight engines arranged in pairs, producing 12,000hp in a

TOP: **As the Spitfire represents the Battle of Britain, so the "Bear" is a Cold War icon.** ABOVE: **The Bear stands tall, 12.12m/39ft 9in high. Note the refuelling probe on this Tu-95H, the ultimate bomber variant.**

tractor and pusher configuration. The eight TV-2 engines, effectively pulling and pushing the aircraft simultaneously, were powerful enough to get 95/1, the Tu-95 prototype, into the air for the first time on November 12, 1952.

The second prototype, 95/2, equipped with four of the hugely powerful TV-12 engines (the most powerful production turboprops ever), was completed in June 1954 and first flew on February 16, 1955. The engines drove contra-rotating propellers, which were used for maximum fuel economy and range.

Production of the aircraft, now formally designated Tu-95, started in January 1956, with the Tu-95M (known to NATO as the "Bear A"), a high-altitude, free-fall nuclear bomber capable

LEFT: **The belly of the Bear, courtesy of a NATO fighter.**
BELOW: **Note the contra-rotating props on this Tu-95H escorted to a UK air show by an RAF Tornado F.3.**
BOTTOM: **The H-model can carry six cruise missile internally, and even ten more under its wings.**

of carrying 9000kg/19,809lb of bombs in its 14.2m/46ft 7in bomb bay over the aircraft's maximum design range. The Tu-95M carried six radar-controlled, turret-mounted AM-23 guns for self-defence. Powered by more fuel-efficient NK-12M engines, deliveries to service units began in October 1957. This was very bad news for NATO because it meant that the Soviet Union now had intercontinental capability.

Most "Bear As" were later converted to AS-3 missile-carrying "Bear B" standard, while around a dozen A-models were converted to Tu-95U configuration for training purposes.

Further versions of the aircraft included the Tu-95K2 "Bear G" which carried two Kh-22 "Kitchen" missiles, one beneath each wing. With a range of up to 460km/286 miles, these 350-kiloton missiles, along with the AS-3, gave the Tu-95 a stand-off capability and improved the aircraft and crew's survivability. The final bomber version of this long-serving but formidable aircraft was the Tu-95MS (the "Bear H"), which carries six Kh-15 "Kent" cruise missiles in its bomb bay and, remarkably, a further ten on underwing pylons.

Maritime reconnaissance variants also appeared while the Tu-142, a dedicated anti-submarine version, was developed with a longer fuselage and a ventral search radar radome. The Tu-142 carries sonobuoys to detect submarines, as well as torpedoes and mines for attack. Ten Tu-142s entered service with India in April 1988 for the long-range surface-surveillance and anti-submarine warfare missions.

An interesting spin-off from the Tu-95 was the Tu-114 airliner. The Tu-95's wing and engines were joined to an enormous fuselage that could carry up to 220 passengers. The airliner debuted at the Paris Air Show in 1959 and entered Aeroflot service in 1961. Thirty examples of the airliner were built, and these served until October 1976.

## Tupolev Tu-95MS

**First flight:** November 12, 1952 (prototype)
**Power:** Four KKBM Kuznetsov 15,000eshp NK-12MV turboprops
**Armament:** Two 23mm/0.9in cannon in tail; sixteen Kh-55 "Kent" cruise missiles carried in bomb bay and under wings
**Size:** Wingspan – 51.1m/167ft 8in
Length – 49.5m/162ft 5in
Height – 12.12m/39ft 9in
Wing area – 297m²/3197sq ft
**Weights:** Empty – 90,000kg/198,090lb
Maximum take-off – 188,000kg/413,788lb
**Performance:** Maximum speed – 828kph/ 514mph
Ceiling – 12,500m/41,010ft
Range – 12,800km/7949 miles
Climb – Not available

# Tupolev Tu-160

The impressive Tu-160 (NATO codename "Blackjack") is the most modern strategic bomber in the Russian inventory, and is the heaviest and most powerful bomber ever. It was designed to operate from subsonic speeds at low altitudes to speeds in excess of Mach 1 at high altitudes. Two weapons bays can accommodate a range of munitions, from strategic cruise missiles, short-range guided missiles and nuclear or

ABOVE: **The heaviest bomber ever built – the Tu-160.** BELOW LEFT: **The "Blackjack" can carry a range of weapons, including bombs, mines and nuclear and conventional missiles. Only 36 were ever produced.**

conventional bombs to mines. Similar in layout to the B-1B, with "swing" or variable-geometry wings, work on the Russian aircraft began in 1973 in direct response to the proposed Rockwell bomber. However, the Tu-160 is much bigger and heavier than the B-1, and can fly faster and much further. The Tu-160 was known to the West even before its first flight on December 19, 1981, thanks to a US spy satellite which spotted the aircraft on the ground at its base. Tupolev built two prototypes and one mock-up, which was used for static tests.

Production began in 1984 and, although initial plans called for the construction of 100 aircraft, when production was stopped in 1992, only 36 bombers had been built due to Strategic Arms Limitation restrictions.

The aircraft is powered by four NK-321 25,000kg/55,025lb thrust turbofans mounted in pairs beneath the fuselage centre section, can climb up to 70m/230ft per second and reach heights of over 18,000m/59,000ft. Terrain-following radar guides the aircraft at high speeds at low level, and all four crew members have ejection seats. The bomber, which is controlled by a fighter-style control column and a fly-by-wire system, can be refuelled in flight using a probe-and-drogue system. The variable-geometry wings can shift from 20 degrees up to 65 degrees and allow flight at both supersonic and subsonic speeds.

The Tu-160 can carry up to 12 Kh-55 long-range missiles and Kh-15 short-range missiles as well as free-fall nuclear and conventional weapons. The bomber is not equipped with any defensive armament, but carries an extensive electronic countermeasures facility.

Deployment of the bombers began in May 1987. Until the end of 1991, 19 Tu-160 bombers served in Ukraine and, on the collapse of the old USSR, the aircraft became Ukrainian property. The aircraft and associated air-launched missiles were subsequently the subject of intense negotiation because Russia wanted the aircraft back. A deal was finally struck in exchange for the cancellation of an enormous gas bill between the two countries.

In July 1999, the Russian Ministry of Defence reportedly ordered one Tu-160 strategic bomber, and the cost was said to be 45 million roubles.

Studies have also been conducted on the aircraft's use as a launch platform for the Burlak space-launch vehicle, which is designed to carry payloads of up to 500kg/1100lb in polar orbits. The launch vehicle would be carried beneath the fuselage of the aircraft, which would give it a head start to a high altitude, thus eliminating the need for excessive heavy fuel loads for launch from the earth's surface.

TOP: **Looking in better shape than the airworthy example opposite, this Tu-160 was photographed in 1999.** ABOVE: **With wings swept and looking like a B-1B, the large Tu-160 can exceed Mach 1.** BELOW: **This large bomber is only in service in limited numbers with Russia and the Ukraine.**

### Tupolev Tu-160

**First flight:** December 19, 1981

**Power:** Four Kuznetsov 25,000kg/55,025lb thrust NK-321 turbofans

**Armament:** Up to 16,500kg/36,316lb of ordnance can be carried in two internal weapons bays or under wings, including six Kh-55 long-range missiles or twelve Kh-15 short-range missiles or free-fall nuclear or conventional weapons

**Size:** Wingspan – 55.7m/182ft 9in, unswept 35.6m/116ft 9in, swept
Length – 54.1m/177ft 6in
Height – 13.1m/43ft
Wing area – 360m²/3875sq ft

**Weights:** Empty – 110,000kg/242,110lb
Maximum take-off – 275,000kg/605,275lb

**Performance:** Maximum speed – 2220kph/ 1378mph
Ceiling – 15,006m/49,235ft
Range – 12,300km/7638 miles
Climb – 4203m/13,780ft per minute

# Vickers Valiant

Designed to satisfy the same specification that resulted in the Vulcan and Victor, the Valiant was clearly a less risky design than its fellow V-bombers. It was this fact that appealed to the Ministry of Supply, who saw the Valiant as a safer, fall-back aircraft should the futuristic Avro and Handley Page designs have failed.

The Vickers Type 660 prototype, WB210, first flew on May 18, 1951, with Vickers' chief test-pilot "Mutt" Summers at the controls. The Valiant (the name was given in June 1951) was a clean, conventional high-wing aircraft with its four engines cleverly buried in the wing roots; their intakes were blended into the leading edge of the wing.

The Valiant B.1 first entered service in June 1954 with 232 Operational Conversion Unit at RAF Gaydon, the first V-bomber base. While the fledgling Valiant crews were trained

ABOVE: **The Valiant prototype, WB210, pictured in May 1951. At this stage the aircraft was the Vickers B9/48. It was named a month later.**
BELOW LEFT: **Painted in overall anti-flash white, Valiant B. Mk 1, XD827.**

(many were converting from the piston-powered Avro Lincoln), the first Valiant squadron, No.138, was formed and became fully operational at Wittering in July 1955.

The Valiant's potential as a long-range strategic reconnaissance platform was spotted early, and 11 B(PR) Mk 1 variants were produced. These could carry up to eight cameras instead of munitions in the bomb bay, although the type did retain its bombing capability. First deliveries of these aircraft to No.543 Squadron at RAF Wyton started in June 1955. A true multi-role version was then produced (14 examples), the B(PR)K.1. Similar to the B(PR).1, this version could also mount a removable refuelling system in the bomb bay, making it a bomber/tanker/reconnaissance aircraft. Total production of all marks was 104.

On October 11, 1956, at an altitude of 10,675m/35,000ft over Maralinga, Australia, Valiant B.1 WZ366 carried out the first air-drop of a British nuclear weapon. The Blue Danube bomb detonated at 229m/750ft and produced a yield of 3 kilotons, equivalent to 3048 tonnes/3000 tons of TNT.

In October 1956, Valiants became the first of the V-bombers to drop bombs (mercifully conventional) when they went into action against the Egyptians. The RAF were keen to test their new strategic bombers in operational conditions, and the Egyptian nationalization of the Suez Canal had presented the opportunity. Valiants of Nos.138, 148, 207 and 214 Squadrons were deployed to RAF Luqa on Malta, and the first Valiant raids against Egyptian airfields were carried out on October 31.

In March 1957, four Valiants of No.49 Squadron were detached to take part in the controversial Christmas Island hydrogen bomb tests. On May 15, Valiant B.1 XD818 dropped a prototype hydrogen bomb at 11,895m/39,000ft over Malden Island. The tests finally proved that Britain had a working high-yield bomb and was indeed still a major player on the world stage. Valiants were also used to air-test and launch scale versions of the Blue Steel stand-off missile that was to equip the Vulcan and Victor.

By 1962, Soviet Air Defences were considered to be too effective for the operation of high-level nuclear bombers, and along with the other V-bombers, the Valiant was switched to low-level tactical operations in 1962–3. While the advanced Victor and Vulcan adapted well to the change in role, the Valiant fleet was silently and literally cracking up. Following an emergency landing of Valiant WP217 on August 6, 1964, examination of this and other Valiants showed that the majority of Valiants had suffered significant stress fractures as a result of operating in harsh low-level conditions. The entire Valiant fleet was grounded while the cost of repairing or replacing the aircraft's spars was considered. With the Vulcan and Victor still in service, the cost of keeping the Valiants flying was deemed to be too high. All Valiants were withdrawn from service in January 1965.

TOP: **WZ395 on approach to Filton, June 1960. The airfield near Bristol was one of Bomber Command's V-bomber dispersal airfields.** ABOVE LEFT: **Valiants were fully operational from July 1955.** ABOVE: **WZ392 was a multi-role Valiant B(PR)K.1.**

## Vickers Valiant B. Mk 1

**First Flight:** May 18, 1951

**Power:** Four Rolls-Royce 4563kg/10,050lb thrust Avon turbojets

**Armament:** Conventional or nuclear bomb load of up to 9534kg/21,000lb

**Size:** Wingspan – 34.85m/114ft 4in
Length – 32.99m/108ft 3in
Height – 9.8m/32ft 2in
Wing area – 219.43m²/2362sq ft

**Weights:** Empty – 34,450kg/75,881lb
Maximum take-off – 63,560kg/140,000lb

**Performance:** Maximum speed – 912kph/567mph
Ceiling – 16,470m/54,000ft
Range – 7242km/4500 miles plus
Climb – 1220m/4000ft per minute

# Glossary

**AAM**    air-to-air missile

**Aerodynamics**    study of how gases, including air, flow and how forces act upon objects moving through air

**AEW**    airborne early warning

**Afterburner**    facility for providing augmented thrust by burning additional fuel in the jet pipe

**Ailerons**    control surfaces at trailing edge of each wing used to make the aircraft roll

**Angle of attack**    angle of a wing to the oncoming airflow

**AWACS**    airborne warning and control system

**Ceiling**    the maximum height at which an aircraft can operate

**Delta wing**    a swept-back triangular-shaped wing

**Dihedral**    the upward angle of the wing formed where the wings connect to the fuselage

**Dorsal**    pertaining to the upper side of an aircraft

**ELINT**    electronic intelligence

**ESHP**    equivalent shaft horsepower

**Fin**    the vertical portion of the tail

**Flaps**    movable parts of the trailing edge of a wing used to increase lift at slower air speeds

**FLIR**    forward-looking infrared, of targeting and navigation

**G**    the force of gravity

**HP**    horsepower

**HUD**    head-up display

**Jet engine**    an engine that works by creating a high velocity jet of air to propel it forward

**Leading edge**    the front edge of a wing or tailplane

**Mach**    speed of sound – Mach 1 = 1223kph/706mph at sea level

**NATO**    North Atlantic Treaty Organization

**OCU**    Operational Conversion Unit (RAF)

**Pitch**    rotational motion in which an aircraft turns around its lateral axis

**Port**    left side when looking forward

**Radome**    protective covering for radar made from material through which radar beams can pass

**RAAF**    Royal Australian Air Force

**RAF**    Royal Air Force

**RATO**    rocket-assisted take-off

**RCAF**    Royal Canadian Air Force

**Reheat**    *see* Afterburner

**RNZAF**    Royal New Zealand Air Force

**Roll**    rotational motion in which an aircraft turns around its longitudinal axis

**Rudder**    the parts of the tail surfaces that control an aircraft's yaw (its left and right turning)

**SAC**    Strategic Air Command (USAF)

**SAM**    surface-to-air missile

**Starboard**    right side when looking forward

**STOL**    short take-off and landing

**Supersonic**    indicating motion faster than the speed of sound

**Swing wing**    a wing capable of variable sweep, e.g. on Panavia Tornado

**Tailplane**    horizontal part of the tail, known as horizontal stabilizer in North America

**Thrust**    force produced by engine which pushes an aircraft forward

**Port**    left side when looking forward

**UN**    United Nations

**USAAF**    United States Army Air Forces

**USAF**    United States Air Force

**USN**    United States Navy

**V/STOL**    vertical/short take-off and landing

# Index

# Acknowledgements

The author would like to give special thanks to Peter March, Kazuko Matsuo and Hideo Kurihara for their help with picture research.

The publisher would like to thank the following individuals and picture libraries for the use of their pictures in the book (l=left, r=right, t=top, b=bottom, m=middle, um=upper middle, lm=lower middle). Every effort has been made to acknowledge the pictures properly, however we apologize

if there are any unintentional omissions, which will be corrected in future editions.

**Alan Beaumont:** 7b; 19m; 20b; 33um; 35t; 37tr; 38b; 42t; 44b; 46t; 48b; 55m; 59t; 65b; 67t; 73b; 79br; 93t; 95b; 103m; 105t.
**Michael J.F. Bowyer:** 58b; 61b.
**P.J. Bryden, Wessex Aviation:** 42b; 73t; 73m; 77b; 105b; 125br.
**Francis Crosby Collection:** 1; 2–3; 4; 19t; 32b; 34t; 36b;

38t; 39bl; 39br; 41tl; 41b; 64b; 72t; 72b; 78t; 114t; 114b; 115t; 115mr; 115b; 124t.
**Chris Farmer:** 48t; 93m; 95m; 112t.
**Imperial War Museum Photograph Archive:** 6b (CL 1005); 21m (FKD 2683).
**Hideo Kurihara:** 53m; 54t.
**Andrew P. March:** 61um.
**Daniel J. March:** 28b.
**Peter R. March:** 6t; 7t; 11tl; 13tl; 17bl; 18b; 19b; 21b; 25b; 28t; 29b; 31b; 32t; 33lm; 33b; 34b; 35m; 35b; 36t; 37tl; 37b; 39t; 39m; 40t; 41tr; 43lm; 45t; 45b; 46b; 47t; 47m; 49ml; 49mr; 49b; 50m; 50b; 51t; 52; 55t; 55b; 56b; 57t; 57m; 57b; 58t; 60t; 61lm; 62b; 63t; 63m; 63b; 64t; 64m; 67ml; 67b; 68t; 69t; 69b; 70t; 70b; 71bl; 71br; 74t; 75ml; 75mr; 75b; 77t; 78b; 79t; 79bl; 80t; 82t; 83tl; 83tr; 83b; 84t; 85tl; 85tr; 86t; 87t; 87bl; 87br; 89tl; 89tr; 91t; 91b; 92t; 92b; 94t; 95t; 96b; 97t; 97mr; 97b; 99t; 103tl; 103b; 104t; 104b; 105m; 106t; 106b; 107b; 108t; 109tr; 109b; 110t; 110b; 113t; 113m; 113b; 115ml; 116t; 116b; 117t; 117m; 117b; 118t; 118b; 119b; 120b; 121m; 121b; 122t; 122b; 123t;

123m; 123b; 124b; 125t; 125bl; 126t; 128.
**Brian Marsh:** 15bl; 107t.
**Geoff Sheward:** 43um; 43b; 69m; 77m; 88t; 93b; 97ml; 108b; 109tl.
**TRH Pictures:** 7m; 8–9; 10; 11tr; 11bl; 11br; 12; 13tr (Ted Nevill); 13bl; 13br; 14a; 14b; 15tl; 15tr; 15br; 16t (Fairchild); 16b (Alan Landau); 17tl (Ted Nevill); 17tr; 17br; 18t; 20t (Colin Smedley); 21t; 22t; 22b; 23t; 23bl; 23br; 24t; 24b; 25tl (Jon Davison); 25tr (Colin Smedley); 26–7; 28m; 29t; 30t; 30b; 31t; 31m; 33t; 40b; 43t; 44t; 45m; 47b; 49t; 50t; 51m; 51b; 53t; 53b; 54b; 56t; 59m; 60b; 62t; 65t; 66t; 66b; 68b (Ted Nevill); 71tr; 74b (Jon Davison); 76t; 76b; 81b (Ted Nevill); 82b; 84b; 85b; 88b (Jim Winchester); 89m; 89b; 90t; 98t; 98b (Art-Tech); 99m (Art-Tech); 99b (Art-Tech); 100t (Art-Tech); 100b (Art-Tech); 101t (Art-Tech); 101m (Art-Tech); 101b; 102t; 102b; 103tr; 111tl; 111tr; 111b; 112b (Ted Nevill); 119m (Guy Taylor); 120t; 121t.
**Nick Waller:** 59b; 61t; 67mr; 71tl; 75t; 80b; 81t; 81m; 86b; 90b; 94b; 96t; 119t.